Positive Pa

and
Communication Skill

---

7 Time-Tested Strategies for Assertive Communication. Learn How to Talk So Your Child Will Listen to You & How to Listen So They Will Speak to You

(Ages 2-13)

Kate Gildon

© Copyright 2022 by Kate Gildon - All rights reserved.

The following Book is reproduced below with the goal of providing information that is as accurate and reliable as possible. Regardless, purchasing this Book can be seen as consent to the fact that both the publisher and the author of this book are in no way experts on the topics discussed within and that any recommendations or suggestions that are made herein are for entertainment purposes only. Professionals should be consulted as needed prior to undertaking any of the action endorsed herein.

This declaration is deemed fair and valid by both the American Bar Association and the Committee of Publishers Association and is legally binding throughout the United States.

Furthermore, the transmission, duplication, or reproduction of any of the following work including specific information will be considered an illegal act irrespective of if it is done electronically or in print. This extends to creating a secondary or tertiary copy of the work or a recorded copy and is only allowed with the express written consent from the Publisher. All additional right reserved.

The information in the following pages is broadly considered a truthful and accurate account of facts and as such, any inattention, use, or misuse of the information in question by the reader will render any resulting actions solely under their purview. There are no scenarios in which the publisher or the original author of this work can be in any fashion deemed liable for any hardship or damages that may befall them after undertaking information described herein.

Additionally, the information in the following pages is intended only for informational purposes and should thus be thought of as universal. As befitting its nature, it is presented without assurance regarding its prolonged validity or interim quality. Trademarks that are mentioned are done without written consent and can in no way be considered an endorsement from the trademark holder.

CONTENTS

INTRODUCTION 9

   DOES KNOWING HOW TO SPEAK MEAN KNOWING HOW TO COMMUNICATE? 9
   HOW CAN I LEARN TO COMMUNICATE EFFECTIVELY? 11

CHAPTER 1: THE IMPORTANCE OF COMMUNICATION . 13

   COMMUNICATION IS NOT JUST VERBAL 18

CHAPTER 2: THE IMPORTANCE OF COMMUNICATION WITH CHILDREN 23

   EFFECTIVE COMMUNICATION WITH CHILDREN IS A KEY ISSUE ... 24

CHAPTER 3: 6 COMMON MISTAKES YOU SHOULD AVOID WHILE COMMUNICATING WITH YOUR KID 27

CHAPTER 4: HOW TO BUILD GOOD COMMUNICATION WITH YOUR KIDS 31

   TALKING ABOUT EMOTIONS 31
   READING AND TALKING 32
   LISTENING 34
   PARENT-SON PHYSICAL COMMUNICATION 35
   CHILD PARENT VERBAL COMMUNICATION 35
   LET'S WELCOME EMOTIONS TOGETHER 36

CHAPTER 5: 4 STEPS TO OPEN A COMMUNICATION CHANNEL WITH YOUR KID 39

   1. ACTIVE LISTENING 39
   2. LET'S PUT OURSELVES IN THE SHOES OF THE OTHER: EMPATHY. 41
   3. GETTING RID OF OR THE "YOU- MESSAGES" 41
   4. PAY ATTENTION TO THE BARRIERS OF EFFECTIVE COMMUNICATION. 42

CHAPTER 6: POSITIVE COMMUNICATION WITH CHILDREN 43

CHAPTER 7: 7 IMPORTANT THINGS TO SAY TO OUR CHILDREN AND 4 STEPS TO GET INTO POSITIVE COMMUNICATION 47

4 STEPS TO GET INTO POSITIVE COMMUNICATION 49

CHAPTER 8: REBUILD A COMMUNICATION WITH YOUR CHILDREN: THE 7 STRATEGIES 55

SEVEN STRATEGIES TO IMPROVE COMMUNICATION WITH YOUR CHILDREN... 56
HOW TO REPROACH CHILDREN WITHOUT DAMAGING THEM 60
HOW TO HELP YOUR CHILD COMMUNICATE BETTER 63
Dealing with critical situations 65

CHAPTER 9: PREADOLESCENCE................................67

Some practical tips for pre-teen parents 73
How to promote positive independence during pre-adolescence.. 74

CHAPTER 10: 10 TIPS FOR MANAGING A PRE-TEEN CHILD WHO HAS BECOME "REBELLIOUS" 77

HOW TO MANAGE PRE-ADOLESCENCE, FIVE TIPS FOR PARENTS 81
MISTAKES NOT TO MAKE: they are not mini-adults. 82
PREADOLESCENCE IN GIRLS 84
DIALOGUE 85
RESPECT HER PRIVACY, BUT NOT TOO MUCH!............ 85
RESPECTING ROLES.. 86
DON'T JUDGE 86
DON'T BE SO HARD WITH YOURSELF........................... 86
PREADOLESCENCE IN BOYS 86
THE IMPORTANCE OF THE DAD.................................. 88
QUALITY TIME. 88
ORIENT, NOT IMPOSE. 88
WAIT TO JUDGE. 88
DO NOT CATEGORIZE... 88

CHAPTER 11: SENTIMENTAL EDUCATION OF PRE-ADOLESCENT CHILDREN: WHY AND HOW TO TALK ABOUT IT. 89

FIVE REASONS WHY IT IS GOOD TO TALK ABOUT SENTIMENTAL AND SEX EDUCATION WITH OUR CHILDREN 89
FIVE TIPS ON HOW TO DEAL WITH SENTIMENTAL AND SEX EDUCATION 92
9 THINGS TO KNOW ABOUT OUR SON'S FIRST KISS 94

CHAPTER 12: HOW TO SURVIVE A PRETEEN CHILD: 6 NEUROSCIENCE-BASED TIPS 107

THE ROLE OF ADULTS 108
TIPS FOR PARENTS BASED ON NEUROSCIENCE DISCOVERIES 108

CONCLUSION 111

BONUS 113

INTRODUCTION

Does knowing how to speak mean knowing how to communicate?

Every human being develops the ability to speak in the first years of life. Language distinguishes us from every other living being and allows us to perform different functions: expressing our needs, experiences, ideas, dialoguing, learning, and obtaining information. Over time, language is enriched and becomes an effective tool for building vital networks of relationships and responding to different situations in life.

However, V. C. Luxury, in "Dynamisms and Obstacles of Interpersonal Communication" (Erickson, 2013) states that in many situations of social life, we communicate badly and do not use the potential that language offers us to manage interpersonal relationships and conflicts better. The first reason is that the quality of communication is closely linked to the quality of the interpersonal relationship.

This is the case with all those situations where there is a lack of mutual listening, misunderstanding, aggression, etc. If there is a relational conflict beyond words, then communication will also be conflictual. In fact, as the second axiom of communication states, there is a plane of content and a plan of relationship in every communication.

The problem is that sometimes we focus on what we are saying and forget about how we feel in that relationship and how we are communicating.

In addition, other components can interfere with the ability to communicate, such as difficulty managing emotions like fear or anger; lack of motivation to make communication effective; learning a dysfunctional communication style; lack of awareness of one's communication style.

Take, for example, the case of a person who has to speak in public and who speaks too fast. Although he may be prepared on the subject and know how to speak perfectly, the message may not reach his audience, who may be distracted or not understand what he is saying. Behind this behavior, there may be a strong emotion of anxiety, or a lack of motivation to want to be present at that moment, or finally, he may have learned to speak very quickly, perhaps imitating an educational model.

In any case, the lack of awareness prevents effective action. Let's consider, then, a second point: we often forget that interpersonal communication skills can be learned, while there is a kind of belief that once learned to speak, the rest is just a matter of character. However, there are many examples of children imitating their parents' way of speaking. Modeling is, in fact, one of the fundamental processes of learning.

This leads us to reflect on how important it is to pay attention to this aspect during the child's development, always respecting what they feel, think and do, and providing them with a good model to imitate. This applies to every age: in fact, Lusso reports that interpersonal communication skills can develop throughout the lifespan and that the most significant development can occur in mature age.

In fact, when the individual has overcome the egocentrism typical of childhood, has accumulated a sufficient number of experiences, and built a broader vision of himself and the other, he can open up to more complex forms of communication. In short, if you can say that you learn to speak in the first two or three years, the rest of your life is to learn to listen and communicate

How can I learn to communicate effectively?

From these reflections therefore comes the raison d'être of a communication book: a way to help people understand how to modify some aspects of their relational style, learning and experimenting with more functional strategies, which are suggested by the different theoretical approaches. Communication is, in fact, behavior and as such, is observable and modifiable. However, communication is not a simple behavior: it involves, in fact, a certain degree of awareness and intentionality and a process that involves several social subjects.

That is why interventions cannot be directed to analyze only a single communicative act isolated from its relational, social, and cultural dispute.

That's why there are no predetermined formulations that reveal the secret of communication to us. Learning effective communication skills involves, first and foremost, a reflection on oneself and interpersonal dynamics. In addition, it involves commitment and intentionality, as the relationships themselves are complex.

Often, when I meet people during communication classes, the observation I am most often made is that all this is difficult, especially since the expectation is to be able to change the other. Instead, communicating effectively is a possible way: but this must start first of all from a knowledge of oneself and availability of knowledge and understanding of the other, together with knowledge of the multiple implications of interpersonal communication.

Assertiveness is, in conclusion, that competence that allows us to recognize one's emotions and needs and to communicate them to others, together with our ideas and requests, in mutual respect, also recognizing the rights and needs of the other.

This requires taking responsibility; it requires exposing yourself and getting involved; finally requires self-confidence and the other. This can be complex, but it allows us to feel consistent with ourselves and establish authentic relationships.

CHAPTER 1: THE IMPORTANCE OF COMMUNICATION

The relationship with children is one of the most complexes in our life, and certainly, being parents is the most difficult job in the world,

> even if it's the most beautiful and rewarding.

As in all relationships, it is essential to establish proper communication between parents and children because only through an effective way of communicating will it be possible to create and carry out a solid relationship with children and give them a gentle and efficient education.

When the children are very young, there would not seem to be any major communication problems with them. The parent generally doesn't even have the problem of figuring out if and how he's communicating with the kid. They usually don't question their behavior and communication because the kid doesn't seem to give them feedback.

In reality, it is important to set up proper communication with children from an early age. There is already the seed of the adult that will be in the child. For this reason, it is important to take care of communication between parents and children even when they are young.

The child forms his personality in the first seven years of his life, and in this period, he learns from his parents everything, the way he thinks, speaks, reacts to life events, and communicates.

If parents do not establish proper communication with their children, they may not be able to communicate effectively and establish positive interpersonal relationships when they grow up, moreover, growing up, there will be difficulties in communicating with the parents themselves.

Scientific studies believe that it is essential to talk to the baby since he is in his mother's belly. Neglecting communication thinking the child is too young to understand what we're saying is a mistake you will pay for later. Alfred Tomatis, a famous French otolaryngologist of the 20th century, highlighted that the intrauterine experience of the fetus has a capital importance in the formation of the future personality and will be, above all, the way of listening and what he will listen to lay the foundations of the individual formal schemes on which the way of the person perceives himself and others will be built and therefore relating to the surrounding world.

The experience of communication starts really early.

Are you sure you are prepared to build solid communication between you and your kids?

Every new parent has doubts and doesn't know what to do in certain situations. Something we all do when we don't have answers is look back in the past to see if we can learn something.

Regarding communication, I don't think the past would help us find our answers. The attention toward communication is quite recent. Families didn't really focus on having a working channel of communication with their children.

That of our parents and even more so that of our grandparents was certainly a traditional family, based on an authoritarian policy. The father was the head of the family, the one who maintained the family united economically and who, for this reason, made all the most important decisions. All other family members had to adapt to them, and no one was excluded.

Within this model, the children were totally subject to paternal decisions, and very little space was dedicated to their thinking, their desires, and, of course, communication.

What was the consequence?

The consequence was, in most times, that family members, especially children, apparently seemed to follow paternal orders, but in fact, they did what they wanted covertly.

That would sound weird and untrue, especially to younger parents, but I know many stories about those dynamics. Women, in particular, had a very hard time having a social life because the threat of a bad reputation was always around the corner. I know stories of some women pushed into marriage even if they weren't sure because of reputation, economy, age, or pregnancy. I know many stories about rebellion against those mechanisms, about children escaping from their own house. Things were really different.

My grandmother was never allowed to hang out with her boyfriend alone, she had to be accompanied by someone who was going to survey the situation. My mother was discouraged from having a lot of male friends, when she got a tattoo without permission, she was almost kicked out of the house.

She tried her best, but the communication in my house when I was little wasn't the best one. My parents were strict, and it was hard for me to make my own decisions, especially when I was younger. They treated me like I was younger than I was because they considered me immature. That made me feel unsure about myself, and that feeling often used to make me make mistakes and mess situations up, which made my parents think I was immature. The circle was not easy to break because the communication channel was not working. I wasn't good at telling them how I was feeling, and they weren't good at listening. Rebellions can lead to dangerous situations. My parents often didn't allow me to do something I really wanted, and I did it anyway. I remember when I really wanted to go to this party because I had a crush on a guy and he was going, such as everybody else in school. My parents didn't want me to go, they never explained to me why so I lied about where I was and went to the party.

I walked alone at night from my house to the party and back even later. I was scared, cold, and lost my way a couple of times before arriving home. If I think about it now, it makes me feel terrible, I will never want my kids to find themselves in that horrible situation. It is way better to communicate, find a compromise, and always be on the same side, a side in which we can keep our kids out of danger, mentally and physically.

I don't want those things to happen to you and your kids. I will help you open a working communication channel with your children, especially during adolescence.

In the last century, we have witnessed the evolution or rather the revolution of the family. We don't have to be subjected to the despotic authority of the father. The evolutionary leap is huge and all the changes happened really fast.

In family law, we move on to the very modern principle of parental responsibility instead of parental authority. In this way, even under the eye of the law, we go over the outdated traditional model to arrive at the modern family model.

It is a family in which the two parents have equal powers and equal rights. Both parents should collaborate in raising children and managing the family, coordinating, and communicating.

The problem of the modern family lies precisely in the inability of parents to manage control collaboratively. A subtle struggle is created between the two in which each tends to want to predominate, making their vision and rules prevail. Another problem might be the predominance of children over their parents. When the collaboration between parents is not on point and they are not able to appear to their children as a strong and collaborative team, anarchy is around the corner.

Anarchy happens because parents do not have an appropriate educational method. They are not united or don't know how to communicate with children to be gentle and loving but also effective. I can tell you that communication is the very core of this method. We will learn in the next chapters how to find this method.

Good relationships are based on communication and respect. Communicating in the family is not always easy, especially if the children are in the critical age of adolescence. Communicating satisfactorily and effectively, however, is fundamental to every human relationship. The secret of communication in the family is undoubtedly the ability to listen to the needs of others, accepting that we are all different and that everyone has their own way of seeing and living things, starting with the little ones.

Let's never forget that even the little ones have their personality, which must always be listened to and respected. The relationship quality between parents and children is much more important than any object the parent can give to the child. It is not material things but the quality of human relationships that determine our full happiness and fulfillment. This applies to all kinds of relationships, including the couple's relationship.

We begin to communicate in the family, especially with the child, even before birth. In fact, the child begins to feel the mother and the outside world in the womb. At birth, the baby's cry is one of the first forms of communication between mother and child. At those cries, the mother often reacts with gentle and loving attention. The newborn then learns to trust others, an indispensable attitude for the future adult, in order to create valid interpersonal relationships.

Communication is not just verbal.

The first communication between child and parents occurs mainly through body language, even when we use words. Whenever the child's way of acting corresponds to our desires, our smiling gaze and tone of voice communicate our approval and joy to the child. And vice versa, our serious expression communicates disapproval. We should be careful about the non-verbal communication of young children, especially if they don't speak yet.

When children cannot speak, non-verbal communication is everything we have on their part. That is not true for us tho. Many parents make the mistake of not using verbal communication with their younger kids because they don't think they can understand. By doing so, you will waste a lot of time you could have used building a working communication channel.

Even if the baby can not understand the meaning of what we are saying, it is precisely by listening to our words that the child finally learns to speak. And with how much joy we listen to his first words! Unfortunately, we often lose interest in his words soon after. Maybe because of the frenzy of modern life, maybe because of lack of awareness, or because we think we already know what he wants to tell us.

A child is a continuous surprise. It is not an extension of the parents, it is not even a doll or a small animal incapable of understanding and wanting. He is always a person, even when he is small and unaware. And as such a parent has to treat it as a different person, distinct from parents and constantly evolving. Therefore it is important always to maintain a good dialogue and good communication. Communicating in the family does not just mean talking, maybe with lectures and recommendations. It mainly means listening and acting as a consequence of what we have listened to. Unfortunately, due to not listening, we sometimes risk making big educational mistakes.

A good relationship based on trust and dialogue with children is essential to be able to help them in case of problems. Not being able to listen to a child when he wants to talk about his adolescent problems can push the son to look elsewhere for a point of reference and guidance. The advice he gets can have bad repercussions and he could be pushed in a dangerous situation. That's why communication between parents and children must be constantly taken care of and grown together with the awareness and autonomy of the child.

Parents have from the very beginning the important task of giving children rules that allow them to integrate positively into the social world. There are many ways to give a teaching, making sure that the parent's voice is a confident guide and not a single source of reproach is fundamental for children's learning. For example, it is very different saying to a child: "baby, you have to sit well on the couch or your back will hurt" than saying, "I told you to sit well on the couch!!! I don't want to see you sitting like that ever again!!!"

When possible, explaining why we are giving certain roles will help your kid understand your point of view and consider what you are saying, not like a despotic use of power. In this way, the baby will be keener to listen and follow the role. We will talk about this later in the book because it becomes essential during adolescence. When the children are older and more independent, the rules also change, but usually, the parents have the last word. However, it is important to dialogue and negotiate with children, find mediations that bring children closer together, and make children understand the meanings that are below the decision taken. Giving roles is the hardest part, but the role of the parent is not just about it. Some parents tend to forget that and talk to their kids just to give them roles. I have often heard kids say, " they only talk to me to reproach me and tell me what I did wrong".

Family is not about that.

We have to do things together and not just household activities. Living and experiencing leisure and not just obligations together, this is the key! Find what kind of experience you like doing as a family and insert it into the family routine. It can be watching old movies together, playing minigolf or any other sporting activity, going out of town, road trips, or playing hide and seek. The kind of activity depends on the family components' age and personality. We will suggest some activities to try later in this book.

You need a working communication channel even to decide what kind of activities you like to do as a family. That can be tricky, I know. The problem in communicating often is that family members don't know or can't ask for what they want. Kids are often unable to tell us directly if they need attention and affection or some time alone. Communication can change many things but only for those who know how to be sincere and honest with themselves and others. Not knowing what we want or how to ask for it (and this is valid for both kids and parents) can lead to family discussion,

In general, family discussions are more intense than those that take place in other areas (for example, in the work area). Family discussions tend to be more emotionally engaging, members feel free to say anything they think, and, due to the close relationships the members have, it is easier to get hurt. People feel freer to assault each other verbally. We have to accept that family discussion will eventually happen. One of the biggest mistakes you can make is avoiding talking about things because you're afraid of discussions. You can not avoid them. Sometimes it is necessary to discuss. You have to teach your kid not to do so too. When topics in the family are considered taboo that cannot be discussed, family relationships can worsen and generate long-term negative consequences. The suggestion is to treat all topics sincerely. This does not mean imposing ideas since there are no absolute truths, so it is useful to communicate using expressions such as "I believe" or "my opinion is".

Communicating in the family is an activity that must be taken care of and cared for day by day. This applies to the relationship with the partner and also with the children. To maintain trust and also an educational relationship with children, it is necessary to listen to them every day. It is vital to have dialogues in the family. A dialogue that is made at the table telling each other about the events of the day, and never letting your children lack caresses and hugs. Children need love, especially when they don't deserve it! Communication allows us to relate to each other. Creating meaningful relationships is one of the fundamental needs of human beings. Interpersonal relationships are essential to the development of the Individual and attachment bonding is an innate need. For this reason, when communication begins to become difficult, the relationship and consequently one's psychological well-being suffers.

CHAPTER 2: THE IMPORTANCE OF COMMUNICATION WITH CHILDREN

Of course, communication goes through different stages, depending on the child's age. Initially, it is about crying. Crying should never be understood as a whim but as an expression of a deep need and not a "vice". Together with eye contact and copying adult facial expressions, it is the first stage of communication of the newborn. Then after some months, we also move on to verbal communication. Therefore, it is up to the parent to support this basic communication of the child, who does not yet have all the other tools.

Supporting your child and understanding what he wants to communicate is the only way the child understands that his thought is received and that he is heard. However, not considering it and ignoring it makes the child feel that his communication is not successful and that therefore, it is useless. This will make your child nervous and frustrated.

Therefore, it is very important to create, on the part of parents, this connection, this expressive bond, which, more than a fact, is a process, a long process, that if cultivated then becomes easy and natural and will last forever. We must never again think that weeping or strange behavior, stubborn demands, or attitudes are an attempt by the child to manipulate us parents or achieve what they want flawlessly. Of course, they test us, but they are simply communicating. We have to talk and communicate with our kids because that's the only way they will develop the tools of communication. We should respect this communication; your kid can't do better. He doesn't have any other tools yet, he is doing his best and we must always listen without looking up, shutting up, or responding annoyed.

Effective communication with children is a key issue.

Every day, the child needs to live stimulating, rewarding, and clear communication situations. Children from an early age come into contact with other children and adults by establishing relationships, communicating regularly, transferring and receiving information. You need to learn to communicate with them properly. The adult person should be able to teach children to communicate effectively in order to correctly solve the difficulties or problems that the person will encounter in his life, without having to resort to physical or verbal violence.

The consequence of such an attitude (that is, the habit of belittling requests or shutting tears away simply as "whims" or requests for meaningless attention) is long-term: by behaving in this way we cannot then complain if, at nine, ten, eleven, twelve years old and so on our children develop closed, arrogant, silent, resentful (depending on the disposition and family situation).

It's normal: if children, as children, didn't feel listened to and weren't used to talking and being really taken into account, they grow up feeling neglected. Communication should first be understood as the line between the world and the human being. It is therefore fundamental for people's social health, and when neglected, it becomes really dangerous, as it does not allow the individual to have the skills to be able to express himself in the world (and not only in the family).

Therefore, this communication must be trained from the first months, from the first years. In the parents and children relationship, communication is entirely the responsibility of the parents. The child has an innate need to communicate, if this communication is not trained but is nipped, a short circuit will be created. We have an important mission to do. It is hard and can be scary, but we were gifted with the possibility to create a new human life and the responsibility to give to this new life all the tools to live in this world.

CHAPTER 3: 6 COMMON MISTAKES YOU SHOULD AVOID WHILE COMMUNICATING WITH YOUR KID

Communication represents the essential tool to build, develop and maintain because it regulates interpersonal relationships.

We define ourselves and others with words, but above all, we transmit messages, information, and meanings. We communicate emotions, needs, intentions, desires, and expectations through words. Words are beautiful but also dangerous. We should pay attention to saying the right words and not turning them into weapons.

Communication takes on even more relevant aspects in the relationship with children because it is necessary to calibrate and moderate each message according to their age. Knowing and understanding how the child's brain matures, when it reaches certain skills, and when it can perform certain mental operations can greatly help parents who interact with them daily.

There are, in fact, many communicative situations in which children cannot fully understand the message, grasping only a part of it, and others that are even harmful or counterproductive.

Let's see together what types of communication should be better avoided.

1. THREAT AND BLACKMAIL

They seem like a useful educational tool, but emotionally, they are very destabilizing for children. **Everything is true for children!** Little ones are not capable of understanding that you are bluffing or that you are saying something out of rage. They think that everything you say is true, they take everything you say as literary.

A threat is always taken seriously, and until they understand that this is not the case, you will enter an eternal tug-of-war that distances and creates relational breaks. Blackmail instead leads the child to feel "without a way out", misunderstood, and controlled. In addition, getting co-operation with blackmail is a paradox: children are led to obey to get approval, rewards, or the good mood of their parents, missing the opportunity to understand why doing a certain action is useful, important, and interesting. Using blackmail and threat, you are not teaching them anything, you are just scaring them.

2. VERBAL AND NON-VERBAL DISCORDANCE

Children grasp the non-verbal aspects of communication very well (gaze, tone of voice, posture and movements, facial expressions...). It would be nice to always remain consistent between the content of the message and the way we transmit it. Example: a child shows us his drawing, we are distracted/assorted by something else, we respond with a "wow, it's beautiful ..." said in a bored tone without paying the attention our kid requested.

Our boredom, distraction, and fatigue will come to the baby, making him feel neglected. Sometimes parents' life is really hard, so there's nothing wrong with feeling tired or bored! It would help if you tried to make it explicit: "I really want to look at your drawing, but now I'm busy/tired. Can you wait until dinner and then we watch it together?". In this way, your kid will feel taken into account, know that you want to give him all of your attention, and sometimes waiting for attention is necessary, but it's okay.

3. IRONY and SARCASM

These are very common ways of communication between adults, they serve to play down, minimize, and make dialogue more fun. However, children do not have the cognitive skills to understand it fully. If you say "Do it calmly !!!" to a particularly slow child, he will just be confused. The communication won't be successful because one of the two parts hasn't understood the message. They are certainly not effective and useful communications at least up to about seven years old. Daily irony and sarcasm could arouse embarrassment and shame, impacting the child's self-esteem.

4. DISQUALIFICATION

"It's not true that you got hurt", "Stop crying, come on...", "Nothing happened, it's nothing!"

Although the adult's intention is benevolent and consoling, it is a disqualification of his feeling and lack of communication for the child. Imagine how you would feel if you told someone you got hurt and they say it's not true, or if you feel like crying and they tell you to stop. It's not a good sensation, am I right? So stop saying those things and think of something else to say like, for example, "I'm so sorry you got hurt, it will pass soon, I promise", "if you want to cry, it's okay, but can I do something to help?".

5. DESPOTIC PROHIBITIONS

Everyone will eventually have used phrases like "don't run!" Or "don't yell!" just to see your baby start doing it immediately! These are not challenges to parental authority but limitations due to the functioning of the brain, and it is something that also belongs to adults. In fact, the brain works by representations so naming the action "running" immediately activates the representation of that action. It's hard to resist if we're two, or three years old...It's better to use positive phrases "Please slow down", and "Can you lower your voice?"

6. JUDGING THE PERSON

"You're a mess!", "Don't be a fool!", "You're rude" are all judgments addressed to the child, to his person, which leaves little escape and are heard as verdicts, making your kid sad or rebel. It's better to criticize actions and behaviors (when it seems necessary to us): "You made a good mess here!

Now let's fix it, come on. Remember to be careful next time, please." The message's meaning is: I always like you, I may not like your actions sometimes.

CHAPTER 4: HOW TO BUILD GOOD COMMUNICATION WITH YOUR KIDS

TALKING ABOUT EMOTIONS

Being able to communicate our emotional states to children is an attitude that can lead to great benefits, especially with the understanding that children mature concerning their subjective feelings.

Learning to discriminate against anger, sadness, fear is a fundamental step, but it is equally fundamental to understand that all this can be communicated (without feeling embarrassed, rejected or turned away) and "used" sensibly and consistently: if I am sad, I seek comfort; if I am scared, I walk away. Telling children how we feel and how we feel may seem strange at first, but it can quickly become a habit of the whole family and turn into something natural and spontaneous.

"I'm really tired today, I worked a lot today, and I couldn't stop. I need a ten-minute break." The goal is not for children to take care of our tiredness (it is normal for them to protest our pause requests!) But make explicit what we feel and what we need. This helps children understand others, the world, and therefore also themselves.

For those interested in the subject, I point out two fundamental texts for understanding empathetic communication: Marshall Rosenberg "Words are windows or walls") and Thomas Gordon's "Effective Parents". The first deals with "Non-Violent Communication", and the second with "Active Listening": both perspectives are of valid help and recognized, taught, and studied internationally. In the field of parenting and Sweet Discipline, they represent two points of reference to change the way they pose and tell their children to help them in their cognitive, emotional, and interpersonal growth. Working on the way we communicate with children at school and in the family (but also at work, with friends...) can really make a difference in the meaningful relationships of our lives.

Speaking in a respectful, empathetic and welcoming way to children is an attitude that helps a lot in the small daily difficulties and that gives real moments of emotional harmony with the little ones, who constantly ask us to help them understand and understand each other (thanks to their constant and intense curiosity about every big or small thing in the world).

READING AND TALKING

As research published by Oxford University Press notes, most parents stop reading fairy tales to their children when they reach the age of 7. A mistake and a waste given the high educational value of fairy tales. Reading stories about animals, nature, and so on together with children stimulates their imagination and intellectual abilities and, above all, allows parents to strengthen their bond with their children and share a moment of leisure with them.

But, alongside reading, another activity further promotes the development of the cognitive abilities of the little ones and improves their communication skills: talking to them constantly. This emerged from a study conducted by a group of researchers from the UK Economic and Social Research Institute and the University of Limerick in Ireland and carried out by interviewing the parents of almost 8,000 children aged only 9 months.

Through the responses of mothers and dads regarding the type of educational and communication activities carried out with their little ones, the researchers concluded that continuously talking to children throughout the day, for example, while doing housework, increases their communication skills and solves problems.

While reading increases the knowledge of new words and develops a positive attitude toward books in children, talking to them continuously increases their ability to communicate and solve the different situations that occur day by day. Those are so many important reasons to converse with your children and involve them in the conversation from a very young age, and do not stop reading their fairy tales!

When they are very young, children learn to speak through three learning tools: sounds, words, and gestures. That's why even a song can have an important effect, and enter the child's head until it gives him full knowledge of a few words. Words must be transferred step by step, and here too it is important that the child can absorb them by hearing them spoken several times. Finally, gestures are decisive in accompanying sounds and words. Two years are an important step in the growth of children's language. It is the moment when the vocabulary of the little one begins to get rich, as far as the eye can see. How to make it rise? And how can we keep a high level of communication with them? The most suitable instruments are: games, songs, and in general music, reading, and facial mimicry. At this stage, numbers, videos, cartoons, and films that deal with nature and in particular, with animals are helpful. After that, around the age of 3, comes the time for board games.

You don't have to be paranoid about children's communication. Some are more discreet, reserved, and shy. Those kids start talking with some delay, but that doesn't mean they don't communicate or, worse, they don't understand. The development of children's language begins between 2 and 3 years: with the first stage, the number of words produced is at least 50; with the second, the perimeter of the child's language widens, and by a lot. And only from this moment, and even better around the age of 4, do we have to start worrying if the child's language is too poor.

LISTENING

Dialogue, the ability to listen, and the propensity to take into account the emotions and the feeling of the other, are essential tools for constructing a healthy educational relationship capable of generating a constructive exchange between child and parent. The parent's main task is to allow the boy or girl to express themselves safely in a non-judgmental and open dialogue.

The natural desire of children to explore the world must not be hindered, perhaps because they are convinced that they must be protected. Still, it must be accompanied by giving them the certainty that the parent constitutes a safe port, the place to return to whenever they need to be welcomed and protected. The more the parent-child bond is built on the safe but not intrusive or hindering presence of the former, the more the latter will acquire security and a desire for autonomy.

The success of this educational system passes through communication, both physical and verbal. Through an open, sincere, and judgment-free relationship, children, even very young ones, can live their emotions peacefully and become conscious and empathetic adults.

Children's emotions are the same as adults; they can feel anger, joy, fear, sadness, disgust, and surprise just like adults. The possibility of being able to express them freely, through tears, screams of joy, or anger, will be the first step to accepting them all and learning to live them peacefully.

PARENT-SON PHYSICAL COMMUNICATION

Physical communication is something that is ancestral, it belongs to our deepest being, and it is nothing but a desire for containment, care, care, and contact. Welcoming a boy or girl in your arms, stroking him, massaging him, and carrying him in the headband, allows a very powerful bond and non-verbal communication. What will happen is that the future adult will be more confident and will feel free to express themselves because they grew up in a protected, warm, but not oppressive situation.

CHILD PARENT VERBAL COMMUNICATION

On the other hand, verbal communication manifests itself through reading aloud, dialogue, storytelling, saying, and recognizing one's own and others' emotions. Parents will be the first to have to show the little ones how to build open dialogues with each other, in doing so, they will know that in case of need, they can ask for help without any fear.

A boy or girl who has experienced love, care, and welcome will be an adult capable of giving this to others. Only by being welcomed can we be able to welcome and never before have we needed women and men able to practice love.

LET'S WELCOME EMOTIONS TOGETHER

The primary emotions, as mentioned above, are happiness, sadness, fear, anger, disgust, and surprise.

Here are some suggestions to welcome them together:

- **Happiness**: boys and girls, already from a very young age, experience emotions all on their own. Happiness can be expressed with screams, runs, and much more. Let's let it out; repress it, maybe because you are in a formal and quiet place, it could be harmful because we will unintentionally block it. We should leave the children free to express themselves, and we respond to their joy with ours, taking only care that the expression of this feeling takes place in the safety and respect of any other people present.
- **Sadness**: also, for this emotion, we should allow expressions. We should teach our kids what fragility is because each of us faces and will face difficult times, and a cry or outgo of emotions will help us to free ourselves in part from sadness. Let's remember that there are no negative and positive emotions, they are all a reflection of what happens around us. We should focus on the manner of manifestation of those emotions, which will be strictly linked to our ability to recognize them and know how to deal with them immediately.
- **Fear**: Fear of dark or loneliness are pretty common fear among the little ones. We don't have to grow brave and invincible. Sometimes if a child is afraid, there is nothing wrong with hugging him, telling him that we understand him, and holding him tight for a while; the fear will slowly go away, knowing that there is always someone ready to be close to us. Suppressing this emotion risks generating a feeling of inadequacy in the child. Adults are also afraid of many things, but they

have learned to overcome them. Tell your kid that being scared is normal and that you still are afraid of some things. Showing yourself to your children for what you are, helps them feel closer to you and allows you to convey to them the appropriate tools to manage the emotion they are experiencing.

- **Anger**: More than fear, anger needs to be recognized, accepted, and channeled. Repressing it can be counterproductive. A parent should try to be welcoming to the child, even during manifestations of a seemingly NOT positive feeling. Reproach and judgment result in frustration, dialogue, and openness to the little one tends to ease the tension. A hug often is much more effective than many words. Being told, moreover, what has upset the child can help him focus on the problem; it can make him clearly feel the adult's attention and thus help him calm down. The child needs to accept his emotions in order to learn how to manage them.
- **Surprise**: Let's be fascinated by this emotion. It's the one we feel in front of something unknown. If we welcome it, it will not turn into fear of the unknown, and indeed, it will make us live intense moments, even of joy.

Kindness and sensitivity to minors help ensure their protection. From this assumption, the still very topical "Guidelines of the Committee of Ministers and the Council of Europe for Juvenile Justice" were written on 17 November 2010. It is no coincidence that justice has also embraced the principles of dialogue and mediation, precisely to protect minors, because only by changing the terms of the relationship, only by understanding and embracing the power of dialogue, understood as recognition and respect for emotions, will it be possible to build a more just and welcoming society.

CHAPTER 5: 4 STEPS TO OPEN A COMMUNICATION CHANNEL WITH YOUR KID

1. Active listening

The first thing you need to know to communicate effectively is to use "active listening" toward the child.

Active listening consists of reflecting on what the child wants to tell us without adding anything else. Active listening is essential to becoming people capable of learning information and responding with appropriate and suitable messages to the situation we are experiencing.

We will not have to override our voice to that of the child or move expressions of dissent or even judge, we should listen to understand; in this way the child will feel free to express himself.

Of course, feedback from the adult is needed to make the kid feel that they are listened to and understood. We will talk again about active listening later, and see how it becomes more important and complicated during adolescence.

How can we put active listening into practice?

A. Passive listening (silence).

It is a silence of openness, you should really be interested and accept everything your kid has to communicate.

Silence is really important in a conversation because it's fundamental for the communication between the two partners to be fluid. Passive listening allows the child to expose their problems without being interrupted and prevents the adult from incurring the twelve communication barriers.

B. Messages of welcome.

Messages of welcome tell the kid that the adult follows him and listens to him. They can be nonverbal attention hints and verbal attention hints. Nonverbal attention hints are about constant eye contact, nodding, smiling... using other body movements indicating that you're listening, etc. Hints of verbal attention, concern words and sounds, small exclamations like "Oh!", "Mmm...", "I understand ...", "I listen to you ..."

C. Facilitating expressions (encourages).

Some expressions invite the child to talk, to deepen what he is saying. Let's be careful not to judge the child; facilitating expressions are something like "It's interesting ...", "How about talking about that part?", "Would you like to tell me something more about this problem?"

D. Real active listening. I listen.

The adult should receive the child's message without expressing his own personal opinions. In this way, the child feels the object of attention, does not undergo negative evaluations, and grasps the adult's acceptance and understanding to solve his problems on his own.

Let us always remember to take time, watch, listen and reflect: we understand and then communicate in the most effective way!

2. Let's put ourselves in the shoes of the other: empathy.

A further fundamental aspect of communication is empathy. Let's try to understand our children, listen to them, try to understand their troubles, and, above all, try to put ourselves in their shoes. Children who are understood while talking about their emotions will learn to be more empathetic.

To do this, observation is fundamental to know him; we can observe what he does, how he moves, how he interacts in the environment and practice learning to read the messages he is sending us to understand his world. In fact, children mainly communicate what they hear!!!

Empathy and children's behaviors

In the behaviors and reactions of children, we can read their desires, fears, emotions, and realities. Children most in difficulty manifest discomfort with behaviors that we adults sometimes do not tolerate, or tolerate only in part.

Learning to value these messages allows you to gain valuable insight into what to do to help them. We can understand how children's behaviors develop through this perspective, especially "problematic behaviors".

To understand children, we will have to temporarily put aside our perceptions of reality, and our usual way of attributing meaning to events and situations. Let's abandon the idea of wanting to confirm our doubts about the likely "difficulty" of the child we are observing.

3. Getting rid of or the "YOU- messages"

We usually communicate with children using the messages the "YOU messages" that are sentences like: "You are like this ..."

"You did not ..." "You should behave differently ..." with the result that the child does not feel welcomed, but judged. The effective alternative to "YOU messages" is the use of "I Messages".

The use of the "I messages" allows adult-child communication based on the absence of evaluation or judgment, but puts the child in front of the effects and feelings that his act causes in others. The "I message" allows the adult to manage a tiring situation. For this reason, parents and educators will have to replace the "you- messages", which places the child at the center of attention, with "I-messages" where the adult is at the center, with his needs and emotions. For example: "When you behave like this you make me angry and I am afraid to lose my temper!" So let's shift the child's attention to his behavior and the consequences it generates.

4. Pay attention to the barriers of effective communication.

Thomas Gordon, a supporter of effective communication and the importance of active listening, believes there are barriers to effective communication. In fact, very often unwittingly, mistakes are made that worsen communication with the other.

Too often the "language of non-acceptance" is used, called "language of rejection", which is opposed to effective communication. These barriers to communication are an obstacle to the dissemination of information, leading to non-acceptance of the child's problem by pushing towards passive and inactive listening.

CHAPTER 6: POSITIVE COMMUNICATION WITH CHILDREN

Words have weight, and those we utter in anger are often the heaviest and most harmful.

However, we must also pay attention to the phrases that parents often say to their children without thinking, without the intention of hurting, without evaluating the damage they could cause. Let's see some categories of phrases said without thinking that they could cause harm in our children without us realizing it.

1. ***Phrases that question our love for the child.*** These are phrases that often come out of our mouth unknowingly, phrases that we do not consider harmful because we know how much love we feel towards our child, we know that this love is indissoluble, indestructible and cannot be doubted. We cannot even imagine not loving our child, however, as we have already explained, this does not apply to children.
Children tend to take everything we say literally and not having a good knowledge and adequate experience of human emotions can really think that a parent can stop loving their child. These phrases are, for example, "if you keep doing this I don't love you anymore!" or "behave well otherwise I don't love you anymore", "today you behaved badly, I don't love you", "when you are good I love you.
2. ***Phrases that make children feel a burden,*** such as "but why did i make children!", "If you want to feel

comfortable, don't have children". "It was a hard day, don't take too much time", "since you and your sister were born, dad and I have only been talking about you", "you are lucky to have parents who go out of their way to give you everything". We always remember that it is not the children who decide to come into the world!

3. Phrases that have the sole purpose of criticizing children such as "you could do more", "you are too lazy", "you do not know how to do it", "you are not capable", "I do it, it's better, forget it".

What are the effects that toxic phrases like these have on children?

First of all, *lower their self-esteem.* The self-esteem of children and young people is fragile and must be built, not demolished. If your children feel like a failure, they will probably become one. In addition to this, the child might:

- withdraw into himself,
- become reserved,
- avoid you,
- interrupt or not build an open and constructive dialogue with you
- fall back on a defiant attitude towards you,
- behave as he believes you see him,
- have a fear of relating to others for fear of being treated in the same way.

If his parents don't believe in him, why should he or others believe in him? If his parents don't love him, how could others love him? If his parents consider him a burden, surely others will too.

This is why it is essential to give the right weight to words.

Communicating positively with children requires such effort that sometimes we feel tired, unmotivated and we question if what we are doing is effective or not.

It's normal to have such feelings but remember to calm down and take a short break from everything in order to get the picture clear. It's normal that kids sometimes don't listen to us, that they have problems and we are the last one to know about them, that they are not very good at handling situation but don't ask for help. I know that and I know how hard parenting is. Calm down, it's not like that every day.

Positive communication means tearing off the forked tongue that would like to spit poison at every emotion it feels and use the power of the word kindly, effectively, directly in a way that never hurts anyone.

What does Positive Communication with children mean?

Positive communication is first and foremost a choice. There is always a choice and we should remember that. When we throw a things in the air, we scream or tell our son that he is bad when he tells us something wrong he did we are making a choice.

Words come out of us. The emotions are ours. If we can't control what we hear, we can choose which words to use. Every choice has some consequences and we can't avoid those. If you want your kid to talk with you about his problems, if you want an effective communication you can't choose this violent responses. The consequences of being angry or violent or not prone to listening is that the kid will be afraid of you and won't come to you to communicate if something happens or how he feels.

Positive communication with children is an act of kindness towards ourselves and our children. It means understanding that through what I communicate (verbally and not) I leave a message that will greatly affect my son.

Think about it:

how much can the things change and growth in the life of a child who is told

- "Thank you" instead of "It was your duty",
- "You dropped your plate, please clean the floor" instead of "You're a disaster",
- "I expect you to do your homework before dinner" instead of "If you don't do your homework, forget your friends"?

No need for an answer, right?

CHAPTER 7: 7 IMPORTANT THINGS TO SAY TO OUR CHILDREN AND 4 STEPS TO GET INTO POSITIVE COMMUNICATION

It is normal that in everyday life, while we look after a thousand things: children, work, family, life as a couple, we often go in such a hurry and are so stressed that we forget to take care of the spirits of our children.

For this reason, I wanted to make a small list of 7 phrases that we sometimes take for granted but which are precious and can make a difference in the growth of children.

1. I missed you.

Often in the happiness of meeting our child again after many hours of work we forget to express this beautiful feeling, the lack. Telling our son that we miss him makes him understand that we love spending time with him and we always want to do it, that when we are not together we always think about him because he is important to us and we really love him.

2. I like being with you

For every parent this sentence can be taken for granted and instead it is nice to remind our children that we spend time with them willingly, that we are happy to have them at home, that even if we are sometimes stressed we are happy to be parents and the choice we have made .

3. I love you so much even though I'm tired

When we appear visibly tired, impatient, nervous and stressed, children often tend to think that it is their fault. Let us reassure our children, do not leave them alone to torment themselves unnecessarily. We remind them of the good we want them and that life as parents, even if it is tiring, repays us for every effort made.

4. I love you even when I scold you.

This is another thing that is taken for granted for parents but often not for children, especially for those who are often reprimanded. It is important to make it clear to your children that when we scold them we do it for their good, that we don't like their behavior, not them.

5. Don't beat yourself up, try and try again.

It is important to raise our children to become determined adults who are always ready for any challenge. Parents in this process must play the role of those who encourage them from day zero, seeing their abilities even before they do. We teach our children that with willpower, by trying and trying again, they will get wherever they want to go! We teach them that failure is only an opportunity to do better and achieve success in small steps.

6. Never be ashamed of who you are and what you think

There is nothing more beautiful than freedom. We teach our children the freedom to be who they are, to think in a completely autonomous and original way compared to any other person in the world. It is important to teach our children to wear their clothes with pride and never renounce their roots, ideas, or beliefs. Life is only one and it shouldn't be wasted playing someone else's shoes.

7. I trust you

Trust is the most important ally of love. Trust must certainly be earned and cultivated, but giving trust to our children will make them feel loved and accepted and make them more responsible and careful not to disappoint us.

4 Steps to get into positive communication

Let's see the four steps to start a new way of communicating based on respect, listening and the equal dignity of all interlocutors. Let's open ourselves to positive communication to improve to bring children back on the same level as us.

1. Emphasize strengthens

It works in such a simple way that you won't believe it.

Many times we limit our communication with the child to statements such as: "don't jump on the couch", "don't eat with your hands", "don't leave your toys all over the house". As i said before talking about how children's brain is made, if you say those things, his attention will flow precisely to that behavior we are trying to eradicate. The denial that precedes action only reinforces action. Moreover, we leave the child without resources, we only tell him what should not be done.

Instead, it is important to start communicating what is important to do. All families have a set of acceptable rules, values, and behaviors. You should explain that to your kid, so when he does something that is against those rules you can remember him that he's not supposed to do that and ALSO tell him what he should do instead. For example, if you told your kid before that in your family no one is allowed to heat with hands, whenever you catch your kid doing it just say " Don't you remember, darling? we eat with a fork, let's go clean your hand and then start to do it in the right way".

"Don't jump on the couch" puts the focus on *jumping* and *sofa*. "You're supposed to sit on the couch," instead, you indicate the right behavior, then you can add "If you want to jump you can jump on this pillow."

In this way you are not only telling him what is the right thing to do on the couch, but also you are recognizing the child's need to move and you're trying to accommodate it with an acceptable alternative. Maybe your kid won't be able to tell you how amazing this new style of communication is but you will see its wonderful effects in the future.

2. Use Horizontal Communication.

How do we look on our children? Are we on their shoulders directing his life or next door, ready to intervene when they need it?

Vertical communication is the one that falls from above, just like you're a movie director on a tall chair. The communication between your boss and you at work is a vertical communication. Do you have this kind of communication with your family? take some times to answer. If you have, you should probably get rid of it. Have you ever experienced this kind of communication? how made you feel? I think that some answers might be "bad", "angry", "frustrated", "sad" "nervous" ECC...

Vertical communications are those that do not consider the other person, do not care about emotions or needs. A child who feels "forced" to do something can react essentially in two ways.

The two Rs:

- **Rebellion**
- **Repression**

Do we really want this kind of relationship? Do you realize how dangerous the consequences can be?

We are still talking about children (even if everything we have just said is at the basis of communication and further we will talk about those same things but with specific examples) but during adolescences rebellions can be wild. Communicating horizontally means perceiving that our child has needs and the request is never imperative. You should respect your children, listen to their opinions and problems, you should be their confident and the person who won't judge but help.

3. Let's talk about our emotions

But why do we want our children to do or not do certain things?

Why do we want them to help us clear, not climb the terrace or leave the newborn sister alone?

Let's ask us those apparently silly questions for a second. We should ask ourselves those questions because our kid asks himself the same questions and we should be able to answer.

When we ask our kid to help us clean, he wonders why we have to do such a boring thing when a second before he was playing with his beautiful toys. It's normal that we want him to help us because we are tired, we have many things to do, and he should learn how to keep the house clean for his future.

Do you think that he knows all of those things? is it automatic?

it's not.

We should explain all of those things to our kids; it's important to talk about our emotions because understanding someone else's emotions without words is not easy for adults, so it's nearly impossible for little ones.

"I'm afraid you might hurt yourself", "I feel very frustrated when you interrupt me" are some sentences that you can tell your kid instead of "stop running" and "don't interrupt me!". The explanation you are giving will make him listen to you and behave because he now finally knows why you're asking a certain thing.

Children will understand that our words are motivated and do not fall from above ("because I say so"). In addition, this way of communicating teaches the child the ability to stay in touch with what he feels and shows him how to communicate it. When your child keeps doing THAT thing they shouldn't do, before getting angry and scream, try to say something like: "I feel very angry when my things are not respected. You can use your fake phone or play another game."

<u>4.</u> Describe what is beautiful you see in him everyday

Dry question: Do you make more praise or criticism of your child?

Let's start here. Often parents find themselves in long lectures about how and why their child should behave "well" and so on but then they are unprepared when it comes to praise.

Every child has a quality to praise. Every child at least once a day does something worthy of our praise. We should not praise nonsense, randomly or too much, what we should do is emphasize the beauty we see in our kids without judgment.

Work on praising specific behaviors. "Oh how good!" "But how beautiful is my baby?!" "You're best of all" are all nice things to say but they are not so useful in terms of education and also, sometimes they might seem fake. Your kid will feel more loved if you praise a specific behavior because he feels that you're really giving him attention and, moreover, he will continue to do what you praised to make you happy.

"You really committed to setting up", "I really appreciate that you let us talk", "I was excited to see you help your sister with homework".

Using descriptive praise means emphasizing with strength and emphasis what the child has done without making a judgment on his identity. It's not a matter of being good or bad. That he is good and deserving of love must be an intrinsic fact in the relationship. Praise also passes from the graces you say to your son, from the enthusiasm you convey, from being an authentic person who reveals the joy of sharing a piece of life together with him...

CHAPTER 8: REBUILD A COMMUNICATION WITH YOUR CHILDREN: THE 7 STRATEGIES

When you are used to yelling at children, communication is the first thing that gets worn out. Having effective, active, and calm communication with your children is essential for the child's growth.

Establishing effective communication with your children is as fundamental as it is difficult. It takes a lot of work to build a channel that can effectively connect you whenever it is necessary. How can we build this channel? It is important to start from childhood so that it accompanies the child during growth and is consolidated in the most difficult moments, namely adolescent ones.

How do you create this channel? How can we improve communication with our children? How can we do it even with children who find it more difficult to express their thoughts and emotions?

Don't blame your child if he can't express his emotions to the fullest, not even many adults can. Some people find it very easy to talk about things that do not have to do with the realm of emotions, such as funny stories, sports news, shopping, world events, books, history, but it is much more challenging to open up about incidents that they perceive as embarrassing because they are more personal. Imagine how difficult it must be for a child to tell about how he was made fun of in school or being scared of something that others might consider silly. Talking about your feelings is complex, yet not impossible.

There are some strategies for parents to help create the right time and use the right tools to allow a child to say what he thinks.

Seven strategies to improve communication with your children.

1. **Before communicating, listen**. Sometimes we spend so much energy finding solutions that we forget that sometimes the best solution is the simplest: listen. Children and adults often just need to be listened to; maybe they don't want to, aren't ready, or don't need advice. Just listening is not "too little". On the contrary, it is the most important step of all, it is at the base of every mechanism of action. If we don't know how to listen, how could we ever learn to communicate? in fact, communication is not one-sided.
By listening, the child gets used to sharing his emotions, knowing that he is heard and never judged, misunderstood, or not understood. Initially, maybe we should push ourselves towards listening, that is, to convince our children to talk by ensuring them our most sincere listening. Then, if your listening is effective, the baby will tend to contact you more often on their initiative. How can you have pure and effective listening? First of all, you must keep your opinions to yourself. I know this can be difficult, but it is best to keep them to yourself, process them, and communicate them only if the time is right or required.

If you feel the urgent need to give advice, perhaps because the situation the child has come up with is really dangerous, you must first make sure that you have listened well and understood how the child is feeling to find the right plan of action. Furthermore, only if the children feel genuinely understood, they are willing to accept the advice parents provide.

Listening, understanding, and re-elaborating before speaking are small tricks that lead the child to develop a strong trust in their parents and their relationship with them. This will make it easier for them to open up and share their thoughts with those who love them the most: their parents.

2. **_Always accept the opinions and emotions of your kid, even if you disagree with them._** If the child does not feel accepted by you, his mom or dad, he will obviously tend not to open up to you anymore. We must therefore accept our children's emotions, even when we do not like them. In fact, accepting does not necessarily mean agreeing with something. It is normal that some emotions of our children make us feel uncomfortable, sad, or even angry but remember that there are no right or wrong feelings, that emotions cannot be controlled and that everyone has their way of living experiences.

Consequently, phrases such as "I don't understand why you are sad, you have a lot to be grateful for!" or "You must not be angry about these things ..." would make the child believe that he is the one who is wrong with something. In addition, these phrases to our children's ears sound like absolute judgments. If our children feel misunderstood or judged, they will tend not to ask us for help anymore. But, how can you push your children towards different emotions? The right and effective strategy is to accept our child's emotions and provide a different point of view. Our children have very little experience, so it can be challenging for them to expand the boundaries of their thoughts. It is essential to use the right words, though, for example, you could say, «I understand this thing made you so angry. But, why don't you try to think that ..."

3. ***Learn the meanings behind your kid's silence.*** We are so used to relying on words that we do not understand that sometimes silence says more things than a well-articulated speech could do. Therefore, we must learn to listen to silence to understand what the child is feeling, even before listening to what the child has to say.

   Silence is very often a reaction to a specific event, for example, it can be used as a way to punish parents for being angry, as a strategy to protect themselves because they are afraid that what they have to say could be misunderstood, or a way to live a painful experience. When children barricade themselves behind the wall of silence, parents often feel frustrated. Still, it is important to understand that silence is not always a symptom of something serious, so you just have to let it happen: even children need intimacy, and this must be respected.

4. ***Create special moments.*** We need to find a moment, even a brief one, where we can be alone with our kid and do something special. These moments shouldn't be sporadic or occasional, but rather regular and constant. These moments could be interrupted by small unforeseen events. If the phone rings, you have to ignore it: in this way the child understands that their relationship has a high priority for the parent. These

opportunities may be occupied by having the child do what he likes most, except competitive activities, as he may feel rejected if he is unsuccessful. Some examples may be: "On Saturday afternoon, a short bike ride with dad", "Talk to mom for 5 minutes before falling asleep," or "Talk to dad while playing with Legos."

5. **<u>Share your opinions and emotions.</u>** Since there are two of us when communicating, it is also important for parents to share their emotions and opinions. In this way, the children will no longer misunderstand certain behaviors or attitudes: if the mother comes home angry about something that happened at work, the child - not knowing it - might think, «Mom is angry, I must have done something wrong! ".

To avoid this unjustified suffering in the child, the mother might say, "I am very annoyed by the discussion I had with my colleague." Talking about one's emotions and specifying them allows the child to recognize the emotions of others. This skill will be essential for any relationship that he will entertain in the future.

6. **<u>Separate the behavior from the child</u>** - Remember to praise or condemn the behavior rather than the child. "I admire how you completed the science project on time" is much more rewarding and specific than saying: "How good you are! My good boy!". When one disapproves of the child's behavior, one must expose one's notes without brutal attacks that devalue the child as a person.
So, instead of scolding him with "I already told you! You are a disaster! », It is preferable to say, « You are wrong in not respecting the rules ». Comments directed at a positive or negative behavior are much more specific,

accurate and effective than those directed at the person, resulting in less devaluing.

7. ***Appreciate different personalities***. Each child has a different nature and, at the same time, also a different way of expressing their emotions. Some children are quiet, some are theatrical, others are rational, others are sensible, and others have little concern and interest in sharing feelings.

If parents fail to appreciate these individual differences, they sometimes turn children into something they are not, resulting in parents feeling frustrated and children misunderstood. Once parents understand their child's way of being and expressing themselves is, they will have to develop a communication approach that best matches the child's needs. In this way the communication is simplified and becomes more pleasant for both.

HOW TO REPROACH CHILDREN WITHOUT DAMAGING THEM

We need to clarify a concept immediately: as much as we try to avoid it and solve every problem even before it arises, we will have to scold our children. Knowing their temperament, that of other family members, fitting them together, establishing rules, deciding the consequences if these are not respected, are all activities that will minimize the reproaches that we must address to our child. Remembering to stay calm, don't scream, follow the five steps will help us make scolding an educational time that doesn't harm our children, that is constructive and non-destructive.

Unfortunately, it is easy to make a reproach destructive. Children, even the most lively ones, are sensitive and cannot get the full picture of situations. If they see you angry at them or hear you scream, they will automatically think that you don't love them anymore, that you don't appreciate them anymore, which could be unbearable for them. That is especially true when we continue to treat them in a different and cold way after the screams, causing them to think that they will never be loved or respected by you again. I know it seems impossible to you, for every parent it is nothing short of unthinkable even the idea of not loving a child anymore, but children having so little experience of life and social interactions tend to take things literally.

When we punish them, use physical discipline or scream we make them feel like a creature who has been rejected for being "evil." If your child feels bad, especially when compared to other quieter brothers or sisters, he will tend to behave like one.

The tantrums, the crying, the screaming, the feet stamping on the floor, banging the head against the wall, breaking things can be gestures of desperation of a child who feels lost after having, in his opinion, lost love and the esteem of his parents. These reactions frighten us and very often we react by yelling, scolding the child further, plunging both of us into a vicious circle.

Think about your situation, did you and your baby end up in this circle? Does the scenario just described seem familiar to you? Do you recognize it in your house? is what always happens? Fortunately, it is possible to remedy, it is possible to learn to scold children so that they learn discipline and common sense, make them responsible enough to recognize their limitations and yours, their needs and yours. Therefore, it will be easier for them to relate to people, limit their demands, tone down and moderate their temperament, and learn to work in a team.

To live in today's society and be integrated, respected, well-liked and productive, they need to be able to recognize the value of authority, an authority that imposes and enforces the rules. For this reason, it is sometimes necessary to reprimand children, because they must learn to behave in line with established authority, avoiding inappropriate, harassing, rebellious and counterproductive behavior.

Bringing them back to order, reminding them of the rules, illustrating the consequences of their actions are necessary actions and are all those that together form a good reproach. Once the child has understood the message of the reprimand, there is no need to go ahead, deliberately harm him, use bad words and non-constructive comments because they disappointed us or made us exaggerate.

Make sure he truly understands and takes seriously the message you want to send. If you see that this has not happened, do not warm up, do not scream and say "I tried, she did not go well, she will never be able to understand in this way". By doing this you will make the child feel wrong, bad, not enough, a lost cause and you could increase his oppositional behaviors because, having convinced himself that you consider him bad, he will really begin to behave as such. If the message has not been properly understood, repeat it in different, clearer words, keeping calm and confident.

The results are to be obtained only in this way: through serious, calm and rational speech. Do not establish a system of rewards and punishments with your child. In this way the behavior that your child should normally engage in would be rewarded as extraordinary, never prompting him to do something truly remarkable. On the other hand, the punishments are often seen as blackmail or revenge.

If you are not good at scolding your children without shouting, first prepare a general speech that you can customize depending on the occasion.

Start with a positive affirmation, as we said at the beginning of this book. Through this positive affirmation you must communicate to the child that he is not bad, that you still love and value him and that you are trying to help them precisely because he loves him and it is your priority to grow up healthy and polite. Then explain which action is not suitable for appropriate behavior and why.

It is important to always explain why we are making such a request to the child, in this way you will also put rationality in front of the anger and the child will be able to understand the deep reasons for his mistake. At this point the child may feel mortified and ashamed of his behavior. Tell him that everything is fine and that there is a remedy for everything, just adopt the right behaviors.Conclude the speech with "peaceful" statements such as: "I'm glad you understood and you won't do it again" or "I'm sure you didn't want to, next time you'll pay more attention to it." "You're a good child, you won't do these bad things anymore, I know"

How to help your child communicate better

Communicating effectively allows children to establish positive and rewarding relationships based on collaboration and mutual help. In addition, effective communication gives them the opportunity to choose to share interests, intentions, emotional experiences and needs with their peers. At the same time, in order for this ability to best develop, it is very important to be willing to welcome the feelings of others, showing interest in their thoughts and desires.

In fact, if a child is adept at communicating, he will certainly be more appreciated by peers and they are more likely to seek his company.

Observing how the little ones interact with each other can certainly help adults become valid guides able to set a good example and enhance the different aspects of communication.

Children can be taught the importance of listening and paying attention to what they are told without interrupting the conversation inappropriately and asking questions when the other stops talking. Communicating refers not only to verbal language but also to body language. By observing people's gestures and behaviors you can guess their moods and intentions. So if we want to teach one child to listen to the other, we can, for example, ask him to focus on his words, without getting distracted.

How to show interest and understanding?

This is where our body comes into play with facial expressions and posture. These are powerful communication tools capable of saying even without words being spoken. We can therefore help children use this type of language just when listening, starting from watching their partner speak and then nods to consent. Similarly, appropriate facial expressions make it possible to make the understanding visible as reported by the other, such as a smile or a movement of the eyebrows in response to a certain comment.

Dealing with critical situations

There are some situations where children may feel insecure, be afraid of each other's reaction, and have difficulty expressing their needs. For example, when they make a request to a friend or classmate or when they want to say no.

In making a request, it is important to help the children communicate in a clear and honest way what they want, giving voice to their needs and taking care to respect the response of others: the other, in fact may decide not to consent. You could then think together about what are the possible ways to start a conversation in which you want to ask for a favor: "I would like…" / "I would need…" / "I would love if…" / "You could…" are in fact all courteous expressions in which you openly communicate your needs.

Likewise, children can be taught to say no sincerely, respecting their desires and those who made that request. You can then once again reason about what can be the most suitable formulas to communicate your will, firmly without raising your voice. Here are some examples: "I'm sorry but I can't" / "I'm sorry but today I can't come to your house" / "I can't lend you notes today, but I can give them to you tomorrow" / "Now I prefer to make this game".

Knowing how to communicate allows children to manage even difficult situations in the best possible way. For example, criticize a comrade or receive a criticism, accept a rejection, apologize, or disagree. Helping children communicate effectively means supporting them as they practice to empower this ability. Help them as they train to listen, ask, reject and say, both with words and with the body, respecting themselves and others.

CHAPTER 9: PREADOLESCENCE

The changes in puberty are physical, sexual, social, mental, and emotional, but when does the delicate phase of preadolescence begin.

How can we help our children in this period of great change? Preadolescence, when does it start?

Puberty begins when changes in the brain cause the release of sex hormones. In general, this happens in females around 10/11 years, but the range is between 8 and 13 years, in males between 11 and 13 years, but may vary between 9 and 14 years. We do not know when these hormonal changes will begin, which are the main stimulus to social, emotional, and physical transformation.

During puberty, most children will experience:

- oily skin (with the well-known acne)
- greasy hair
- increased sweating and body odor
- the growth spurt (about 11 cm per year in girls and up to 13 cm per year in boys).
- The changes in mood

Mood changes and changes in energy levels are normal circumstances in puberty, as is the continuous oscillation between the willingness to become independent of parents and the demand for support from parents.

The pre-teen wants to establish and fix his own identity, which could lead him to create new friendships and social relationships, to have difficulty managing the current friendships, even those long-standing that have accompanied him throughout his childhood, want to explore their sexuality develop the first romantic relationships.

And again, at this stage, our children need:

- seeking more responsibility,
- take care of your appearance and your look,
- Preserving their spaces and privacy.

How to help them?

At this age, boys and girls can alternate being self-conscious and feel omnipotent after a few hours. These are common and completely normal changes that show that our child is transforming, is facing one of the most extraordinary transformations of life, and is becoming an adult. It is forming its own identity and experimenting with the pros and cons of independence: it tests its decision-making skills and learns to recognize and understand the consequences of its actions.

One of the best strategies that we can put in place during the puberty of our children is reassurance: they are normal changes, and even if they can scare will pass and represent fundamental stages to becoming adults, to transform the cocoon into a butterfly.

Let's encourage them to take care of their body, especially because it is important to keep it healthy, and take care of their appearance without exaggeration or fanaticism. We should offer them a healthy lifestyle.

Your daughter is becoming a woman. And your child's body is preparing to become that of a man. Even if boys and girls become more and more independent at this age and yearn to make choices with full autonomy, the presence and collaboration of parents are very important. Here are some tips.

Your daughter is becoming a woman. And your child's body is preparing to become that of a man. Hair sprouts, hips become rounded, breasts grow, and menstrual periods generally begin. Just as in boys, mustaches and beards start to appear, and the timbre of the voice changes. But being 12-14 years old doesn't just mean having to deal with (big) physical changes: a whirlwind of emotions marks this transition phase in which you leave the childhood nest, and you have to learn to manage the rough seas of adolescence ...

Let's see some challenges your pre-teen has to face:

- recognize oneself in a changing body and accept oneself as different from how it was before
- being no longer children but not yet mature women and men
- conflicts with parents, first crush, first attractions
- the concern of being accepted by the peer group.

Moreover, it is a phase in which the group of friends can be the "viaticum" for the first approaches to alcohol, cigarettes, and sex. Not to be underestimated, then, the anxiety triggered by having a body different from that of the models (female and male) proposed by TV and the risk of eating disorders.

Here are some typical changes of this delicate phase of development, in the awareness of the enormous heterogeneity in terms of physical, emotional and psychological maturity between one child and another.

On an emotional and social level:

- They show more attention and concern for their body image and look.
- They are very focused on themselves in a precarious balance between high expectations and a lack of confidence.
- They experience mood swings.
- They show more interest (and are influenced by) the peer group.
- They express less affection towards their parents to the point of appearing rude or cold, or aloof sometimes.
- They can feel and manifest the weight of school work that is gradually becoming more and more demanding.
- They can develop eating problems.
- They are vulnerable to sadness and depression, which can impair academic performance and bring them closer to alcohol or drugs and unsafe sex...

On a cognitive level:

- They have greater complex thinking skills.
- They get better at expressing feelings through words.
- They develop a stronger sense of right and wrong.

What can you do in this delicate moment?

Here are some tips that the **US Centers for Disease Control and Prevention** give parents to support raising children in this sensitive age group.

- Be honest, clear, and straightforward when talking about sensitive topics like drugs, alcohol, cigarettes, and sex.
- Meet and get to know your son/daughter's friends.
- Show interest in her school life.
- Help your child make healthy choices by encouraging them to make their own decisions.
- Respect his opinions and consider his thoughts and feelings. It is important for him/her to know that they are being heard.
- If there is a conflict, clarify goals and expectations (for example, getting good grades, keeping the room tidy, being respectful), and help them figure out how to achieve those goals.
- Even though they are now small women and young men, mothers and fathers continue to play an important role in safeguarding the well-being and safety of pre-adolescent children.
- Make sure they always wear seat belts when traveling in a car.
- Make sure they always wear a helmet when riding a bicycle, skateboarding, motorcycle, or playing contact sports.
- Discuss the dangers of using drugs, cigarettes and alcohol and unprotected sex. Discuss these issues, listen to what they have to say, and answer their questions sincerely and directly
- Talk about the importance of having friends interested in positive activities and encourage them to avoid peers who force them to make unhealthy choices.

- Establish that you must always know where they are and if an adult is present when not with you. Agree when you need to talk to each other on the phone, where you can find them and what time they should go home.
- When they are home alone, set clear rules: what they can do and not do. For example, if they can invite friends, how to handle situations that can be dangerous (who to contact in case of emergencies, etc.).
- Encourage your children to be physically active.

In addition to practicing some sports, they can help you with household chores:

- Curing the lawn.
- Bringing the dog to walk.
- Washing the car.
- Throwing the garbage.

Those are some activities that contribute to keeping them active.

- Sharing meals is very important. Both encourage dialogue and comparison on their respective days and promote healthy nutrition.
- He limits the time he can stay in front of the screen: no more than 1-2 hours a day would be ideal.
- You should facilitate your children's social life as much as possible, involving them in activities outside the home with other peers and under the guidance of another adult. The children must also live the socialization experience with peers without being guided by mom and dad from time to time. Make sure

they have those experiences, even if you're nervous about them.
- Supervise their life online. This is a very delicate age regarding the use of technologies, so it is essential to pay close attention to their life on the net, where they expose themselves to high risks.
- Find a fair balance between the need to protect children and their need to explore the world. For example, a bicycle is a perfect tool for exploring new city areas. Still, parents often do not allow children to go on bike rides because of an excessive overprotective approach.
- Studying is an activity that involves fatigue and requires attention, concentration, and prolonged commitment, and kids risk being discontinuous and distracted by the frequent use of social media. Make sure that they take their time to concentrate on their study. Then call clear family rules: for example, during the study, they cannot use technologies to focus on reading, repeating, memorizing, and assimilating the contents.

Some practical tips for pre-teen parents
- Praise your child for his efforts, achievements, and positive behavior.
- Put yourself in your child's shoes and try to see his behavior for what it probably is: your child fighting to become an adult.
- Try to stay calm during the outbursts of anger of your child: wait for the moment of anger to pass before talking about what happened.
- Stay interested, involved, and willing to talk.
- Try to support your child in his self-expression, even if some things seem strange to you, such as an extreme haircut or unusual clothing choices.

- Try to tolerate long periods of time spent on personal care, such as hours in the bathroom, but talk to your child about reasonable time limits for the family.
- Talk to your child about any permanent changes they want to make to their body, such as tattoos and piercings, and discuss temporary alternatives, such as henna tattoos (removable).
- Talk to your daughter about your period and how to manage your period.
- Reassure your child that the testicles develop unevenly, and it is normal that one is lower than the other. It might also be helpful to explain that penis size does not affect sexual functioning. I know that sometimes it is hard for us as parents to talk about those subjects but not doing it is harmful.

Our parent's generation would have never talked about something like that but can't you remember how many questions did you have as a teen and the sense of fear and frustration because nobody was there to answer?

It can be embarrassing for you to talk about the size of your kids' genitals, but it can be overwhelming for them to worry about it. Your girl might be insecure about her breasts, and your boy about his penis, which could affect their self-confidence.

How to promote positive independence during pre-adolescence

It's normal for our son to want more independence, but he still needs our support at this time more than ever. Let's talk to him about the risks and how not to put his life in danger while he tries to explore his boundaries. Let's ask him to let us know what he does and where he is. Finally, let's take some time to accept that many things are changing our child, our role as a parent, and the family dynamics.

We no longer have total control over our kid's choices and life, and we can only tell ourselves that we have done our best to prepare him for this moment, that we have confidence in him and in everything we have sown in previous years.

CHAPTER 10: 10 TIPS FOR MANAGING A PRE-TEEN CHILD WHO HAS BECOME "REBELLIOUS"

Until a few months ago, you had an almost idyllic relationship. For some time, your son has assumed attitudes of insubordination, rebellion, and aggression.

What happened? Are we doing something wrong?

Preadolescence refers to a child between the ages of 11 and 14. At this time, children transform physically and start to increase their sexual drive. He\ she gets angry at nothing, refuses to obey, complains about not being understood, and sometimes takes on rude attitudes that make you wonder where he has learned.

1. *In pre-adolescence, it is normal for children to change.*

The change is part of the growth, and it is necessary that, with the arrival of the preadolescence, the child is no longer the obedient child tuned to the parent's expectations as it was until a few months before. Learn to love this new version of your kid. See him more as an adult. He is becoming the person he will be in the future, and this is a hard process. He is growing up, you managed to give him a beautiful childhood and you should be proud of it, but now he's leaving that stage of life, and he's going through a different phase that will lead him into adulthood.

2.Not to perceive their attitude as a lack of affection.

Often, however, parents are disappointed by their children's behavior and perceive their estrangement as a kind of loving abandonment, as if the child suddenly did not love the parent. Love has nothing to do with it and is not questioned.

What the son is looking for with this behavior is to put a sort of barrier of separation from the parent, as if to sanction a physiological process of differentiation from him. Not for nothing sometimes concretely manifests this need by locking himself in his room and putting at the door signs like 'knock before entering' or 'do not disturb' to make us understand that he is different from us.

3. Interrupt communication if it exceeds the limit.

In this separation process, anger and insubordination can be there. Still, the parent must remain an adult, maintaining a calm attitude and not letting himself be tempted by the impulse to enter the dispute. If your kid cross the line by raising his voice and getting aggressive, we should interrupt the communications, saying that we don't want a fight but a conversation and that we are ready to talk when he calms down. This behavior has a strong effect on a pre-teen, who instead would have the desire to continue to provoke or keep the conflict high.

With our behavior, instead, we pass the message that we are open to dialogue about everything, but with regulated tones, without crossing certain limits, and without swearwords. And at the same time, we commit ourselves to do the same with them because the pact of non-aggression must apply on both sides.

4. After the "storm," the situation can be clarified

When his anger has gone out of the phase of greater emotional activation, the child returns to a normal situation. At that point, we do not start preaching, and we do not demand 'from above' an apology, which would be just a gesture of passive obedience. Let us ask him to rethink the words he told us and try to put himself in our shoes to understand what we felt.

We could also write him a note to leave in the evening on the pillow, or, to be more technological, send him a message in which we express how we felt, always in a calm way. In this way, we stimulate him to reflect on it, activate critical thinking, and develop awareness of what has happened.

5. Do not be afraid to say no (for fear of their aggressive reaction).

Even in this phase of the "tsunami" that is the pre-teen, a parent must maintain his role and have the courage to say no. However, what to do if there is a ban that children show they do not want to submit to? In this case, mom and dad must be allies and consistent in communicating to their son that the adult has a clear plan in mind. He must know what yes and no means. Just as it will be necessary to be firm on some points that children claim, in the same way, it will be necessary to be proactive and encourage the spaces of autonomy and freedom that parents have decided to grant to their children.

6. Tolerating the boy's frustration for our "no".

When we say no, of course, we cannot expect them to be happy; on the contrary, they will tell us that we are the worst parents in the world, who hate us and other similar compliments. Let's not collect the provocation; we have to remain calm to show that the authority does not come from who raises the voice more but from who has the clearest ideas. It must be taken into account and is part of the mechanism of brain functioning at this age, which is strongly active in emotional experiences.

7. What to do if they tell us: "you don't understand me".

It is one of the classic phrases when there is a quarrel between parents and children. We can reply with a counter-question: 'if you think I can't understand you, help me understand what I can't understand about you, tell me what you would you like me to hear.' In this way, we encourage the boy to bring out his needs and discuss aspects that he considers misunderstood. Maybe a need arises that we can satisfy, or instead, he comes up with a request that cannot be granted, to which we will simply reply that no parent who cares about their child could ever make such a concession! Sometimes children try to make requests that they already know are exaggerated, but then they feel almost relieved to see that we, as adults, continue to be a solid point of reference even in the no we give them.

8. If he makes the comparison with his brother or sister.

Another classic: 'you prefer him', 'you understand him, you don't do it with me. In this case, let's answer them that we are always the same and they are different, that we are willing to understand both even if sometimes it is not easy. The important thing is to keep an attitude of openness so that the child does not see a rigid parent, who only has the anxiety to defend their positions, but a parent who is always inclined to listen to the child's point of view.

9. Avoid punitive strategies, such as the classic cell phone hijacking.

Hijacking the cell phone makes sense if the 'blame' for aggressive behavior comes directly from the smartphone, otherwise, it could only arouse anger. Better to foresee "additional punishments", which increase commitment and responsibility, such as hanging the clothes for two days and clearing the table for three days. And if they refuse, then let's go back to the classic punishments such as stealing the beloved cell phone. However, let us remember that any punishment must be punishable and comfortable for us too (the seizure of the cell phone means that when our child goes out, he cannot be reached by phone!)

10. Keep in mind that it passes.

This attitude of insubordination lasts all the time of the tsunami of preadolescence, up to about 13-14 years, because it is part of a very precise phase of development of the brain's neuronal system. After the storm, the calm will return!

How to manage pre-adolescence, five tips for parents

Preadolescence can be considered the phase of life in which our body undergoes more upheavals, excluding the nine months that each of us spends in the mother's belly. The main difference is that in the period of pregnancy, we are not aware while, between the end of elementary school and the end of middle school, we are fully aware of what is happening to us. In many cases we end up in an adult semi-body still retaining the thoughts and maturity of a child.

Often children going through this phase are troubled by the change in their bodies and by the social expectations that follow, they succumb to psychological pressure they cannot tolerate. But how can we manage pre-adolescence then? And a preteen child?

MISTAKES NOT TO MAKE: they are not mini-adults.
At this stage, according to various studies, many parents make the mistake, albeit unconsciously, of treating their children as if they were mini-adults. A ten-year-old girl can be bright, intelligent and even very mature, as well as physically structured, but we must not fall into the misunderstanding of believing her to be older than she is. From a cognitive point of view, today's preteens move more casually in the world, as if they were little men and little women. Still, the emotional development remains the same as in previous generations. The main problems to be faced in this age are linked: on the one hand to the forms of discomfort, often deriving from the perception of one's own body, which lead to forms of social withdrawal such as not wanting to go to school; and on the other, the difficulties in observing the rules and recognizing the authority of adults.

1 - Do not mistake them for adults

First of all, as mentioned above, we must not espouse the idea of having adult people in front of us. The best approach is the gradual one that passes through the recognition of your child's maturity without burdening him with too many expectations and responsibilities.

2 - Few but mandatory rules

The famous stakes are essential for charting the high road during pre-adolescence. A balance must be maintained between prohibitions and concessions from school performance to return time. It is right to trust your children and load them with responsibility but you have to do it progressively because a child who is too free can become anxious.

3 - Protect without invading

The parent's job is a bit like that of the tightrope walker, especially when it comes to the privacy of their children. To refer to the most classic of examples, it is not recommended to spy on the girl's phone, even if she has the best intentions of her. It is a real invasion of the field: it is like wanting to be present in a room where your daughter confides in her best friend. The only solution to build a healthy relationship is a direct dialogue in which we try to listen rather than give indications. Pre-adolescents send signals all the time, you have to know how to grasp them.

4- Don't judge

It may happen that your child has become a person you don't like in preteen years. His passions do not convince you and you point it out to him. This is not the right approach because pre-adolescence is the age of experimentation in which children search for their own identity. A parent should be able to suspend judgment and accompany the child to discover the many possibilities available to him

5 - *Give him the tools to get by on his own*

Within physical and psychological safety limits, one must allow one's children to fend for themselves. Dealing with a quarrel with a classmate or enduring a mockery allows the preteen to grow by activating resources that would otherwise remain dormant. We must avoid being too protective. Here, too, the right attitude is that of a wait-and-see who studies the situation and intervenes only in case of real need.

PREADOLESCENCE IN GIRLS

Preadolescent daughters, five tips to know how to behave with our daughters in such a complicated period. Preadolescence is an age of great upheaval for our daughters, from excessive attention to the physical aspect to the need for privacy.

Preadolescence is a journey to a middle ground where the body often begins to resemble that of an adult, but the head is still that of a child. In girls, this "transformation" begins around eight and ends at thirteen. In these years, the forms change, and the first emotional repercussions come with them. Just think that the beginning of this phase is marked by the first menstrual flow, which is a painful experience that can cause discomfort and shame. For some decades, there has been an advance in the times of preadolescence that forces girls to deal with the issue from maturation at an early age, and often, they are not yet equipped with the emotional maturity necessary to deal with it.

The growth, depending on the way and age in which it takes place, directly affects the child's personality, who can take two opposite paths to deal with preadolescence. If they can see that the transformation arouses consensus, they tend to exalt to force social relations, but if their physical appearance embarrasses them, they feel shame and want to remain in the shadows. Both attitudes are difficult to manage. Often, the parent is in the situation of having to find the right key to open the door that these little women, in the first impulse of protecting their privacy, close behind.

DIALOGUE

The first step to establishing a healthy relationship with your daughter is dialogue. To be profitable, the parent must develop his listening skills. Behind the desire for confidentiality, every pre-teen retains the desire to share some areas of their lives. The important thing is that they decide when to do it because the interrogation has never been very successful.

RESPECT HER PRIVACY, BUT NOT TOO MUCH!

When they close the door of their room, the girls still have the internet at their disposal, which is a real window into the world. The network is a source of endless possibilities but also insidious. For this reason, the parent must be able to overcome the challenge of monitoring what his daughter does without being intrusive. Here too, it is essential to maintain an active dialogue. The Internet can be dangerous, especially for girls' self-esteem. Demonizing the internet and keeping her away from it won't work. Instead, what you can do is teach her that what she sees online is not real. You can use the internet to do so. There are plenty of YouTube videos or TikTok showing that what you see on the internet is fake. Search for videos exposing that pictures and videos can be edited and that posing and light change everything.

RESPECTING ROLES
The parent must be a parent, and he must not try at all costs to become a friend of the daughter. Children feel the need for a critical gaze that knows how to set limits even in this situation. Limits are essential for pre-teens and, even if your girl doesn't tell you, they make her feel safe.

DON'T JUDGE
Many parents are disappointed by the sudden change in their children. A child who loved to read suddenly can be more attracted to social networks and television programs that we consider not too clever. In these cases, it is necessary to insist on postponing the evaluation because what is one's daughter at that moment is not necessarily the snapshot of what will be tomorrow. Your girl will be an intelligent strong woman one day, what you see today is just a scared little girl trying to calm the storm she has inside

DON'T BE SO HARD WITH YOURSELF.
Finally, suspend judgment even on yourself. Preadolescence is a problematic age even for parents. You come from childhood, a period during which you could "enjoy" your children fully. Now everything is different and harder. At this stage of their growth, preteens want to emancipate themselves, and it is right to give them a controlled detachment. It will be impossible not to make mistakes, so don't be too intransigent with yourself in this process.

PREADOLESCENCE IN BOYS

Changes, at any stage of life, can break a balance. Even if the novelties introduce an improvement, in the first phase, they leave us bewildered. In pre-adolescence, the transformation factors are so many that they turn into a storm.

Suddenly our children find themselves dealing with a body that they no longer feel and that they cannot control. Physical traits begin to resemble those of an adult more than those of a child but thoughts and maturity remain anchored to a large extent in childhood.

This conflict manifests itself in emotional difficulties that not all children can face serenely. The main problem at this age is managing the exuberance that can lead to aggression. Male pre-adolescence relative to female pre-adolescence occurs slightly later and is usually between nine and a half and thirteen and a half. In this period, physicality explodes, which often vents in moments of instinct and anger that alternate with regression and a return to childhood. We go from bold attitudes, like challenging the world riding a scooter, to those in which a tender and childish side re-emerge. Once they have taken note of the change in their body, many centimeters gained in height and first hair, the boys rise on the social stage of the peer group, or their peers, and show off their new identity.

Early or late physical maturation actively affects the construction of the boy's personality: those who grow up earlier and live the new appearance well, also thanks to forms of social appreciation, tend to be more aggressive and, in some cases more aggressive, those who develop later, usually, it is more reserved and remain in the shadow of adults. In favor of the latter, however, there is the possibility of better managing the transformations on a psychological level because the body begins to grow when the mind has had a few more years of maturation available.

Within these internal conflicts, there is the role of the parent who must be able to accompany his child on this bumpy path.

THE IMPORTANCE OF THE DAD.
The father must take the stage in pre-adolescence. Children's relationship with their mothers is more ancestral, while with their father, they can speak the same language and discuss the new problems that distress them. From pleasing girls to difficulties with friends, this is the right time to open an important sharing channel.

QUALITY TIME.
It is not important to spend a lot of time with your child, even if it certainly does not hurt, but it must be used correctly. It is not always necessary to resort to dialogue to strike the right chords in the male world. Just share moments that strengthen the relationship, such as a concert or a game in the stadium.

ORIENT, NOT IMPOSE.
In the parent-child relationship, it is important to know how to listen. People often make the mistake of imposing their own solutions on growth. It is useless to push a child to play football by claiming "football saved me" if the boy wants to play the guitar. We must learn to observe to find the right way to accompany him on this path.

WAIT TO JUDGE.
Your child is a mess at school, he combines all the colors and often smells of sweat. Don't despair, the mini-adult in front of you isn't necessarily a photo of the man he will be. Give it time to make mistakes and to grow.

DO NOT CATEGORIZE.
In this stage of growth, your children are hungry for identity. Don't make the mistake of labeling them "he's the geek" or, conversely, "he's the plague". These attributions risk heavily influencing the perception they have of themselves. Parental judgments are important to kids, even if they go out of their way to prove otherwise.

CHAPTER 11: SENTIMENTAL EDUCATION OF PRE-ADOLESCENT CHILDREN: WHY AND HOW TO TALK ABOUT IT.

Our children are increasingly informed about sex and more and more early. The main sources of information? Internet and the media in general.

But what they learn from certain sources is not always adequate for their age. For this reason, it is good that parents first talk to him about it, in a way appropriate to their growth phase. It's one of the hardest topics we can talk about with our children. But that we can't overlook because their voids can be filled with distorted information, which preteens learn every day from their surroundings, starting with the internet.

Five reasons why it is good to talk about sentimental and sex education with our children

1. Because the internet and media give information without filters

The media bombards us with images and messages about sexuality understood as pure pleasure of the moment, impoverished of the many emotional, affective and psychological implications it should have. Since childhood, therefore, our children absorb the concept that sexuality is linked to the satisfaction of a momentary pleasure, which does not involve mind and heart. The main source of information for a growing kid is the Internet. Information that can be found on the web is not filtered according to the user's age or level of development, so it happens that the same content, images, or videos can be seen by a novice kid and a sexology scholar. Kids may run into sites where sexuality is made up of violence and perversion, which are presented as normal because he's curious about sex. And in a still immature brain, this creates confusion because what is instead the result of a perverse and sick conception of sexuality risks being perceived as normality.

2. Because we have to teach that love is a path to live step by step

Teaching sentimental education means making the boy understand that sexuality cannot be reduced to the mere encounter between bodies. It is a wonderful experience that involves someone 360 °, in body, heart, and mind. And precisely for this reason, it must be allowed to grow step by step, as the relationship is enriched with tenderness, protection, harmony, and complicity. Choosing and living carefully every "first time", starting with the first kiss, which is like a milestone in a boy's affective growth, and precisely for this reason, it must not be wasted. Every single stage must be lived with emotion, but also with reason.

3. Because physical development is getting earlier

Pubertal development comes earlier than a few decades ago, at an age when the critical thinking capacity typical of an adult mind has not yet developed. Teenagers, Pillai says, have a body that goes like a Ferrari when the mind still rides. A physiological discrepancy since during preadolescence, the brain areas related to emotion (the limbic system) develop very quickly, while the cognitive part, dedicated to critical thinking, is still immature. This means that teens are often at the mercy of their drives and their state of excitement, without being able to think about the consequences of their actions. Also because the more years go by and interaction with peers increases, the more the spaces that children allow us to talk about certain topics decrease. It's up to us adults to help kids train their ability to reflect, starting even before the hormonal storm of puberty arrives and they are overwhelmed by powerful energy like a sexual one.

4. Because gender stereotypes are still hard to die.

You might believe that certain mentality about male and female roles is stuff from the past, but marketing – and pornography – are permeated by stereotypes of men who never have to ask and women who give in to so much power. The boys then receive as patterns of behavior those of predatory males who use females as objects in their hands, who demand everything as if everything were due to them, without respect or negotiation. Girls, on the contrary, receive the message that to assert and gain popularity, they must be beautiful, sensual, and perhaps even available. Girls might think they are worthy only if admired by others and not for the value they recognize in themselves. A culture that can creep dangerously into affective relationships, generating the belief that you need to adapt to scripts imposed by your partner to be loved.

5. With the increasingly early use of cell phones, you live more virtual relationships and fewer real relationships.

Our children are always super connected, and one would think that thanks to this 'social' life, they have many more relationships. Recent research shows that adolescents experience fewer romantic relationships, and later than in the past, they are also more lonely, depressed, and insecure. This is because prolonged technological devices offer fewer opportunities to confront reality and experience true relationships.

Five tips on how to deal with sentimental and sex education

1. Preparing a path from a very young age

You don't have to wait for your child to be a teenager to do sentimental or sex education. A good education can start from when children are very young, with the gestures of everyday life: during the bath or the change of the diaper, for example, you can promote the knowledge of the body, presenting the various parts, including the genitals, as beautiful and important; infant massage, on the other hand, can be an opportunity to discover the sensations of well-being always respecting the emotions of the child and never including actions that can be sexual.

2. Provide the first information during primary school

From the age of 6 onwards, theoretical information on sexuality can be gradually transmitted, which should be accompanied hand in hand by formal activities organized by the school. At this stage, we can begin to explain how the genital organs work, how the sperm fertilize the egg, and how the embryo develops in a fascinating and engaging way. And it is at this age, one can introduce the concept that certain aspects of sexuality can only be lived when one is older, without burning the stages. Indeed, it is good to give the child small rules of self-protection, warning him, without alarmism, that no one can ask him to do, touch or see something that makes him uncomfortable. And, if it happens, he must immediately warn mom and dad. All the more so if asked to keep the secret.

3. Don't miss the questions.

As the child begins to know about sexuality, so many doubts and curiosities can arise, and he might begin to ask us questions. We should not appear embarrassed; otherwise, he would understand that we prefer not to talk about it. Instead, let's try to understand what his curiosity is at that precise moment, with questions like, "Why are you asking me? Where did you hear about it?"

Most of the time the answer is enough to satisfy the moment's curiosity. If, for example, while we see a movie together, a scene of sex and love happens to us and asks us if we also do certain things, simply answer that it is a beautiful thing that all couples who love each other do. Questions like those help us take time and understand what real curiosity he has and decide what to answer without adding more than what he is asking of us and without anticipating information for which he may not be ready.

4. Stimulating dialogue without being intrusive during preadolescence

With preadolescence, you can teach kids what it means to make love, how to understand when you're ready, how important elements such as respect, empathy, and responsibility are, and what implications it can have, such as an unwanted pregnancy or a sexually transmitted disease. They may have less desire to talk to us at this age, but it is good to find opportunities to deal with the issue, starting with a book, a video, or a song. The important thing is not to be intrusive, to know how to listen when they talk to us, without being in a hurry to give our advice. We have to accept their secrets, respect them, and never make fun of them: the message they must receive is that there is nothing that cannot be talked about in the family, even if you make a mistake.

5. Talking about sexuality as a beautiful thing

When we talk about feelings and sexuality, it is important to get our child to get the message that living a love relationship is something beautiful. Remember the emotions you felt when you had certain experiences, and tell your kid how love leads to seeking closer and more intimate contact and how it is from the love of two adults that new lives can be born. An experience so beautiful and precious that it cannot be done with the first one that happens, which takes place only with both consents when both respect each other and are responsible for their actions. So that they too may have a wonderful love and sexual life.

9 things to know about our son's first kiss

Preadolescence is the age at which hormonal storms begin when the first falling in love can be born and the first kiss with the first love can also come out.

But won't it be too early? And how can we parents behave in the face of these first love impulses?

The first kiss is never forgotten. It is one of those experiences that a boy has so much curiosity to do and can't wait to do.

But is there a right age?

1. There is no right age to give the first kiss

What can be said is that it is not unusual to find it during middle school, a phase in which children begin to make the first explorations in the partly still unknown territory of affectivity, under the pressure of the hormonal impulses of adolescence and the example of what they see happening in their peer group.

2. Stimulate the development of critical thinking about what they see

Often children are driven to try certain experiences because they see the example of other friends who have already lived them and with whom they do not want to feel less. In this case, it is important always to keep the dialogue with our children open and invite them to reflect on the fact that what others do must not be a script to which to adapt at all costs, but they must do what they feel suitable for their needs.

3. Don't say yes just because they ask us

Another concept to teach is that we must never enter the dimension of affectivity or sexuality obediently, so the choice to give or not give a kiss or have other exchanges of affection must not be made only to obey the requests of the other, otherwise, it would mean becoming an object, not being the subject of the relationship.

4. The first kiss: the limit not to cross.

At this age, it can happen that a first infatuation results in a kiss. Along the path of sentimental education of the child, the parent must teach that, at their age, there should not be the overcoming of this gesture, which must remain the maximum within an affectively connoted relationship.

5. It's not a game, but it's part of the exclusivity of the relationship.

Another key concept is that a kiss is not an experiment to be repeated many times with as many different people, almost like a workout that, the more it repeats, the more it improves "performance". Love effusions are part of the intimacy and exclusivity of a relationship, in which so many unique and unrepeatable emotions come into play.

6. The scenes in the movies? They are movies!

In the scenic fiction of cinema and TV, it often happens to see love stories that are born and develop so quickly that children are led to think that in reality, it happens like this. It is up to us parents to teach our kids that certain events are exaggeratedly speeded up and fictionalized. In reality, falling in love involves the construction of sequential and very slow affectivity, which needs intermediate passages. And even a kiss is part of a path made up of phases and gradual stages.

7. Responsibility, respect, attunement, empathy

Because a relationship is connoted as effective, it requires the coexistence of four different dimensions that do not develop in an instant but are built little by little: responsibility, respect, attunement, and empathy, which mean that in a relationship, there is not only what one or the other thinks or wants, but there are limits, there is respect for the times and desires of the other, there is the construction of a shared model, in which the same things are tried and desired. These are difficult concepts for a boy to understand because the brain areas where certain mental functions develop are still particularly immature in preadolescence and early adolescence. On the contrary, the area of the emotional brain is very developed, which leads a boy to feel a lot and reflect little. And then act on impulse.

8. A grown-ups body in a children's mind

This immaturity of brain development stands in contrast to the early maturation of the body, which leads, for example, today's girls to have their first cycle much earlier than a few decades ago, with the result that adolescents today have a body capable of doing things that the mind cannot yet support. It is up to us adults to retune our body and mind, making sure that the body takes the time to wait for the maturation of the mind.

9. And when the first kiss comes, they will know how to behave

The process of a child's affective education is built-in dialogue, in a relationship, in everyday life, through what we testify with our behavior and what we have made clear about the importance of the effective - and then sexual - dimension in their lives. When the opportunity comes, and they have to make choices, there will not be a parent present who will tell them what to do or not to do. Still, they will have to have some sort of inner parent and decide the limit of availability they want to put in the relationship.

How to react to the first "love" of pre-adolescent children.

The first loves come well before adolescence. What happens in this delicate age of passage, between the ages of 10 and 11? Advice for moms and dads of pre-teen children struggling with their first crushes. The first heartbeat comes earlier, well before adolescence. And moms know that. But just like children are not always able to decipher that whirlwind of emotions and sensations so different from the more complex ones characteristic of teenagers.

What kind of feeling are we talking about between 10, 11, and 12? Generally, the infatuations, even if lived as falling in love, are short-lived for those children. There is still no maturity for a real deep relationship made up of conscious choices. In today's society, we tend to anticipate all the stages. The world surrounding pre-teens – especially the media world – with its models pushes them to accelerate behaviors once typical of later ages. The first actresses of this change are typically females, who, around the age of 11, start playing the part of older women and talk about love and falling in love.

What do they feel, and what do these former children discover? They mostly borrow adult patterns, use the word "boyfriends" because they heard it at home or from some adult, and the mistake is especially those who involve them in these terminologies so far from their reality. This does not mean that real passions can be felt as early as 3-4 years of age, even for same-sex children, towards whom very intense and sometimes exclusive emotional bonds are established.

Is the best friend a form of love too? Yes, for those who have it, it is a kind of alter ego that satisfies a need of those who are more fragile: it is another self that gives strength to the group. Sometimes those who do not have it build an imaginary friend, always to confide in and confront each other on the same wavelength. Observe from a distance; never be intrusive and interrogate. It is essential to respect your kid's privacy. If your kid wants to talk, let him talk and listen without making judgments. Use tact and discretion. Pay attention to excessive mutism and continuous mood changes, which can be a sign of discomfort to deepen. Avoid teasing him and belittling him for his feelings, especially in front of other adults.

Don't tell family, friends, and relatives around about his infatuation. Avoid formalizing the situation even just for fun. If you invite home what is more than a friend, treat him or her like a normal schoolmate, without differences or allusions. Do not tell your partner about the crush if you know that he would invade the intimate sphere of the child because of his personality.

Sex scenes in movies: how to deal with kids?

You are watching a movie with children that seemed suitable for everyone when a sex scene appears out of the blue. What do you do? Should you look at it anyway? Should you turn the tv off? Should you change channels?

If the scene is too passionate or the child is too young, you should change channels. If you realize that it is a 'hard' scene or a violent one or if the child is under four to six years old, you can always change channels, accompanying the gesture with a simple explanation: "There is a scene that is not good for your age, we did not know it, so it is better to change".

If the child is older, it's better to explain what is going on. If the child is older, it's needless to avoid the subject: he would understand that the parents are in trouble, and changing channels with embarrassment could increase his curiosity ('who knows what is going on!' he will think) or make him think that sexuality is something dark, dirty or ashamed of.

If the child asks us the classic question 'what are they doing?', an answer must be given. You don't need too much scientific explanations or mileage speeches, they will generate even more confusion and send him the message that we are in trouble. Just answer that the two characters in the film are hugging hard because they love each other and they want to make love, which is a normal thing between two who love each other.

Children are much simpler than we adults and need simple and reassuring answers. It is important to use a quiet tone of voice because, for children, the tone of communication has more meaning than the information itself."

What needs to be avoided

- Leave the child alone to see certain scenes.
- Laugh at your question.
- Pretend that you have not heard or understood the meaning of your request.
- Respond that he cannot understand and will understand when he grows up: even if they are small, they do not want to be treated as unable to understand!

Teenagers and preteens: what to do if they tell lies

It is certainly important that the parent educates children to tell the truth. It is vital not only to build a relationship based on trust, but also to accustom them to facing reality and the consequences of what they do.

But telling a few lies is a physiological step toward autonomy...

For our children telling a lie is also a gimmick to assert their autonomy. Younger children do this to experience the thrill of not being totally transparent to mom and dad or to hide some silliness they did. This is especially true when they face preadolescence and adolescence, which mark the phase of transition from parental addiction to the desire to show that they know how to look after themselves, to make choices that would not always be pleasing to parents. It can then be said that lying is a physiological step in the growth process.

Sometimes children hide some truths because they fear they would displease parents or already know that they would disapprove certain behaviors.

So why do they do certain actions anyway?

Because there are experiences they feel they have to do, because they found themselves in a group, because they had the pleasure of doing so, because they know that it would remain an isolated episode and there is no need to worry parents.

We would indeed like them to learn to say no when friends propose dangerous things, but on the other hand, if for years we have accustomed them to always conform to what mom and dad wanted, how can we expect them to have autonomy of thought when they're with friends?

What to do if we notice the lie? If it is small, let's welcome it.

Suppose one afternoon he tells us that he is going to do his homework with a friend, and instead, we discover that they went together to the theater. In that case, we can also accept it by pretending nothing happened because he did not commit anything dangerous after all. Sure, a parent may displease the idea of being ousted secretly, but he must put his soul at peace that it is normal for a teenager to become 'opaque' at some point.

If it is a bigger lie, he must be blamed and punished.

What to behave if it is a more important lie? In that case, we do what belongs to our role as parents, scolding, explaining why he was wrong, and showing our disappointment at seeing our trust betrayed. And, if that's the case, we might need to give certain behaviors punishment, which he'll learn to bear. Our parental task is to educate them on the truth, especially towards us.

How to prevent our kid from telling us lies

First of all, it is good that the parent does not burden the child with exaggerated expectations: failing to meet them, he could be more easily led to hide behaviors that do not meet expectations. For the rest, let's take into account that we can't avoid his lies altogether. Nor would it be desirable precisely because they are indispensable for achieving autonomy of thought.

What if he ends up on bad roads?

In this case, the problem is not the lie but all the education we have given so far, which should have allowed him to build his own 'backboard' of fundamental rules and values from which to draw for all his actions and choices. Once we have well equipped him, we can only trust him while considering that sometimes he will be wrong. We must always watch over "dangerous" lies.

However, some lies can hide risky behaviors that need to be exposed. How? If we realize that something is wrong, that our son is always detached from us, he has a mysterious attitude, his mood is no longer what he was before, he does not want to attend the group of friends of all time, we must be vigilant.

We should try to open a dialogue with him, without attacking, without asking questions, but making ourselves present, expressing our doubts and concerns. Sometimes, the children themselves leave signs of their lies (cigarettes shamelessly forgotten at home), as if they wanted to be caught to get out of a lie they no longer stand. And, the moment they begin to open up, we should not attack them with offenses or humiliations.

We should teach them that you can make mistakes, but you can get out of it; that a lie, even a big one, can always be fixed without feeling at a dead end. Otherwise, they may feel stuck in a situation they no longer have the courage to confess, and the lie risks getting magnified or becoming more dangerous.

Adolescence and preadolescence: how to defend yourself against judgments and criticism?

Gossip, unsolicited judgments, and criticism are on the agenda among adolescents and pre-adolescents, which can hurt a lot. How to help our children defend themselves? First of all, by providing them, from an early age, with a 'safety suitcase' that helps them deal with various situations and endure frustrations. They have to get used to the idea that you can't please everyone and that, when it happens, you can face the criticism. The first step to helping our children face the judgments and criticisms of others is to give them, from an early age, a 'safety suitcase', that is, an education based on the reflection of their emotions, on sharing, welcoming, but also on respect for the rules.

Only in this way, in the course of growth, will they acquire good self-esteem, learn to create good relationships with others, to give the correct value to experiences, even unpleasant ones, that can happen to them. And above all, it will develop resilience, that is, the ability to react in the most appropriate way to various situations and withstand the frustrations that will inevitably result. If, on the other hand, we get children used to feeling like small emperors, they will never learn to handle the slightest conflict and, at the first criticism, they will go into crisis.

Show understanding for his anger and disappointment.

Although we have tried to prepare him over the years when certain unpleasant episodes occur, it is normal for our kid to be disappointed and manifest his anger with us.

What is the best approach on our part?

We should always show compassion for his mood, telling him we're sorry for what happened to him. After that is important to point out that these are things that unfortunately can happen and will still happen, among children and adults, at school, in the workplace, in the sports group, and condominiums. It is up to us to give the right weight to any criticism, even if disappointment is inevitable. If we have something to tell, we can add episodes in our lives where we found ourselves in similar situations to make it clear that we know perfectly well what he is talking about.

Teach him small but effective communication strategies.

What behavior should we suggest to our kid if he deals with negative criticism and judgments? Let's remember our kid that it's needless to take offense or get angry: we would only play into our 'adversary' hands.

One of the most effective communication strategies is the so-called paradoxical answer "to the 'critic'. You can try to say phrases like: 'maybe you're right, let me better understand what you mean, how I should act in your opinion'. In this way, we place ourselves on an attitude of asking for help that immediately pops up arms and lowers the aggression of the interlocutor.

Move the speech on a playful plane.

Another trick that works is to move the speech on a playful plane. Pushing out a witty joke, and using irony or self-irony helps dampen the tones and create an atmosphere of sympathy. Maybe you can do 'technical tests' at home, simulating situations and trying to devise together how you can react. In this way, the boy trains himself to use different communication tools or creative strategies, which not only give him greater confidence but help play down the problem a little.

There is criticism and criticism.

It is also important to make children understand that, since there are many human beings, there are many points of view, and that sometimes criticism can also have a constructive purpose because it can give the starting point to reflect on one's behavior, consider the way of thinking of others and push to improve oneself. We must help them not to let them be conditioned by destructive criticism of those said only to do harm, perhaps dictated by envy or jealousy. Indeed, in the latter case, the best suggestion you can give your child is to assess what source a negative judgment comes from and give 'negative' people the weight they deserve. And, if that's the case, change around because it's not really worth getting lost behind sterile gossip.

Involve the reference figures

If gossip, 'factions', and exclusions arise within the school or a sports team, the best solution is to involve the reference adults, i.e. teachers and instructors. If the teacher is smart, she will be able to speak to her group in the right way and put in place inclusive measures that will allow children to amalgamate with each other and resolve criticism and conflicts in the bud.

CHAPTER 12: HOW TO SURVIVE A PRETEEN CHILD: 6 NEUROSCIENCE-BASED TIPS

Preadolescence is just a middle age. It is suspended between childhood and adolescence, and those who live and cross it live simultaneously the sadness of no longer being children and the desire to grow up. The body of preteens tells this ambivalence well: it changes every day, makes those who possess it tremble with fear and shame because it tightens and widens, fills with pimples, and often presents itself disharmonious both in forms and movements.

Adults remain in disbelief in the face of their child's changes. Middle school time is when preadolescence bursts in and blatantly upsets everyone's lives. Parents must arm themselves with healthy patience in order to manage emotional excesses, the roller coaster of their children's moods, and even the small, large emergencies that children live, unable to make relative what is instead an absolute impossible for them to face. A pimple can lead a beautiful girl to believe she is a monster who can no longer leave the house.

A small stain on your shirt or pants can make you decide never to go to a party you've been waiting for a long time ago. Preadolescents often lack the ability to put everything into perspective, to downsize events: for them, everything happens here and now, and the most feared thing is the judgment of other peers, considered a priority over that of mom and dad.

THE ROLE OF ADULTS

Adults need to stay calm and use an approach that is both reassuring and protective, promoting and exploratory. Without the adult support to go out into the world, some preteens would struggle to leave the house, even just for a short walk on the city's main street. At the same time, other parents are challenged by the preadolescence of their children, who would never stop exploring the outside world and having new experiences, which are sometimes very risky.

The preadolescence of some children, in fact, foresees such a strong acceleration in terms of new experiences and new behaviors that the adult must never tire of guarding the territory of the growth of a child, clearly defining expectations and limits, providing stimuli, but at the same time decisively clarifying rules and boundaries not to be crossed.

Neuroscience has explained very well that a preadolescent's brain is strongly immature in his cognitive part (what he thinks) and highly mature in his emotional part (the one he feels and seeks strong sensations and emotions). That's why everything a preteen child does often seems irrational, exaggerated, and too driven toward seeking excitement.

TIPS FOR PARENTS BASED ON NEUROSCIENCE DISCOVERIES

Here are some tips for adults struggling with the "tsunami" that preadolescence brought to their family or classroom. ***Always consider that a preadolescent's brain first feels and then thinks.*** In preadolescence, the thinking (cognitive) brain is much more immature than the brain it feels (emotional). This is why the preteens' actions are strongly oriented toward searching for strong and intense emotions.

The emotional brain uses, in fact, its "power" to direct the mind towards its own goals, to the point that often, the young subject himself is struck and shocked by this domain. When preteens tell us, "I don't know why I did it," they're not necessarily lying. They often found themselves involved in actions their emotional brains pushed them to do without stopping even a minute to reflect on the implications and consequences that would ensue. It is up to us educators to help them rework their mistakes and predict the behavior to be followed in the future so as not to make mistakes anymore.

Be patient. When entering preadolescence, the functions of emotional self-regulation, motor coordination, and ability to resist frustrations are still very immature, and this forces adults to exercise the art of patience compared to the many messes, mistakes, and unexpected events of preteens.

Help them not to get distracted. Faced with computational, concentration, and impulse control activities, the brain of a preadolescent struggles much more (despite having, in theory, very high abilities) due to the frequent interference produced by the emotional brain, which tends to distract him continuously, making the fatigue and frustration associated with the study unbearable. Therefore, we adults must help preadolescents limit as much as possible environmental interference that can distract and demotivate them. For example, during study time, getting their cell phone out of the way, turning off the television, denying access to computers and video games, etc. might help them.

Let them sleep. Research has shown that the brain's need for rest changes significantly after the age of twelve. Sleep deprivation in preadolescence and adolescence makes irritability and depression more frequent, increases impulsivity, and tends to take risky actions. Getting a preadolescent to sleep as long as his brain needs to recover emotional and cognitive energies is of paramount importance for the boy's psychological well-being.

No to alcohol and tobacco because it is easier to develop addiction in this period of growth.

If your child is angry, **_you should stay calm instead._** A preadolescent in anger needs a calm and authoritative adult to show him what it means to stay in the here and now, to maintain control of the situation, even if you are in the grip of a very strong emotion. If you lose your balance more than him in the face of his anger, yell, throw his cell phone to the ground, threaten him, and tell him words you never wanted to say, you will only accentuate his state of emotional activation.

The goal of educational intervention is the exact opposite: to put the emotional brain in touch with the thinking brain and develop a conscious strategy to overcome the moment of difficulty.

CONCLUSION

I hope this book has helped you understand the importance of communication in relationships with children.

It is important to start building a communication channel with children from when they are still in the womb. The advice contained in the section on communicating with children is all based on a few essential principles for every parent. Among these the most important are never to be impatient, not to scream, not to belittle the child, not to use sarcasm.

Even if they are small and hardly speak, our children understand much more than we think. For this reason we must always treat them as our equals and never as beings unable to understand what we are saying or what we want them to do.

The same thing goes for the rules. It is important to have fixed rules. These rules, however, must respect as much as possible the nature and character of our child, as well as his inclinations and preferences. The rules can be explained!

Gone are the days of "just do it!" "That's it because I said it!" "I don't want to hear complaints!". Explaining to our children the motivations behind certain rules will push them to respect them. Childhood is a wonderful time and I hope that with these simple tips you will be able to fully experience your child's childhood, communicating with him, without screaming, without fights and without punishment.

Pre-adolescence, however, is a complicated time. To communicate well with your child and make him want to communicate with you, you first need to understand what happens. Pre-adolescence is a complicated period first of all for him. His body changes, his hormones go crazy, his way of feeling emotions changes. Everything changes and they are not always ready. Physical change poses numerous challenges for our children. We parents will always see them perfect but in his head getting used to the change is complicated and this can make him dissatisfied with his body. Pre-adolescence today is more difficult than ever.

Social networks have changed everything, everything is more difficult. Speaking of the body again, our children have to deal with unattainable aesthetic models that strongly damage their self-esteem. Having good communication in the age of the internet is more important than ever because your child has easy access to all the information he wants to obtain and you cannot know how it is transmitted to him. It is important that you take matters into your own hands and become his most trusted source of information.

For this you don't have to be afraid to face difficult topics like sex, drugs, relationships. I hope this book has helped you not to be afraid of having difficult conversations. By following these tips, you will build a safe and functional conversation channel with your child. Your baby will feel comfortable with you and will start talking to you about everything!!!

Seeing is believing!

We have the task of helping our children in this difficult moment of their life and supporting them even when they appear rude, distant, always in a bad mood or rebellious. I can assure you that behind these behaviors there is a great suffering and confusion due to the delicate moment they are going through.

Our children need love just when they least deserve it!

BONUS

Dear user, I would appreciate it if you would spend a minute of your time and **post a short review on AMAZON to let other users know how this experience was and what you liked most about the book.**

In addition, as of recently I decided to do a giveaway to all our readers, yes, **I want to give you a gift:** *the audiobook will be totally free for you!*

Below you will find a QR CODE that will give you direct access to this bonus (mp3 files to download directly to your device) *without having to subscribe to any mailing list or having to leave your personal data.*

We hope you enjoy it!

Also, as a publishing house, we have many more books that perhaps might be of interest to you or your loved ones in various genres (for example, cooking).

If you would like a copy, if there is a problem downloading the files, or if you simply want to share your opinion with us directly, we will be delighted to hear from you: write to author.author1001@gmail.com

A friendly greeting, we wish you the best

Printed in Great Britain
by Amazon